The Edge
of
Every Day

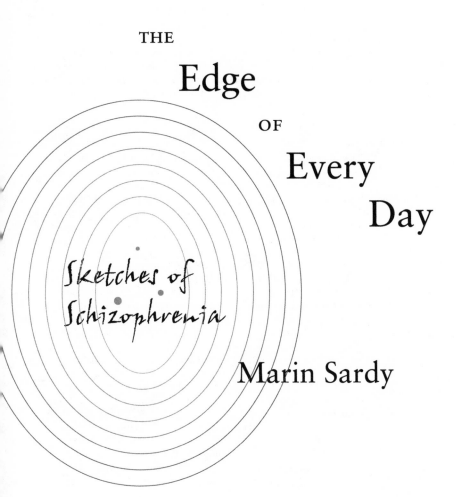

THE

Edge

OF

Every
Day

*Sketches of
Schizophrenia*

Marin Sardy

Pantheon Books, New York

All rights reserved. Published in the United States by Pantheon Books, a division of Penguin Random House LLC, New York, and distributed in Canada by Random House of Canada, a division of Penguin Random House Canada Limited, Toronto.

Pantheon Books and colophon are registered trademarks of Penguin Random House LLC.

Some chapters in this book were originally published, in slightly different form, in the following publications: "Strange Things I Have Encountered" in *The Crooked House* (2012), "A Shapeless Thief" in *The Missouri Review* (2014), "Chokecherries" in *Phoebe Journal* (2013), "The Dragon at the Bottom of the Sea" in *Fourth Genre* 18:2 (2016), pages 153–66, "Disintegration, Loops" in *Post Road* (2014), "Dades Gorge" in *Madcap Review* (2014), "Theory of Mind" in *Puerto del Sol* (2016), "All My Charms" in *Cactus Heart* (2013), "Animate" in *Hobart* (2015), "There Is the Urge to Find Meaning" in *Sweet: A Literary Confection* (2016), "Break My Body" in *Guernica* (2016), and "Nix" in TheRumpus.net (2016). "The Rumor" was originally published as "Upright Eggs" in *Bayou* (2014), and "A World of Absolute Order" was originally published as "Lightning, or Feathers" in *Tin House* #68 (2016).

Library of Congress Cataloging-in-Publication Data
Name: Sardy, Marin, author.
Title: The edge of every day : sketches of schizophrenia / Marin Sardy.
Description: First edition. New York : Pantheon Books, 2019
Identifiers: LCCN 2018042987. ISBN 9781524746933 (hardcover : alk. paper). ISBN 9781524746940 (ebook).
Subjects: LCSH: Schizophrenics—Biography. Schizophrenia. Schizophrenics—Family relationships.
Classification: LCC RC514 .S3155 2019 | DDC 616.89/80092 [B]—dc23 |
LC record available at lccn.loc.gov/2018042987

www.pantheonbooks.com

Jacket design by Kelly Blair

Printed in the United States of America
First Edition

1 2 3 4 5 6 7 8 9 10

For Adrienne

These notes are directed
towards a region
I wanted to perceive
but could not.

—BHANU KAPIL,
SCHIZOPHRENE

Contents

The Edge

of

Every Day

Strange Things
I Have Encountered

THE PATTERN I SAW AS A SMALL CHILD WHEN I CLOSED MY eyes: concentric ovals in purple, red, and electric blue, the oval rings vibrating around a few dots in the center, which vibrated too.

The sound of my mother sitting on a sofa in our quiet house late in the evening, rhythmically grinding her teeth.

A halibut's migrating eye after it has worked its way around to the other side of its head, where it is not quite aligned with the rest of the face.

The ash that fell from the sky and coated Anchorage in gray dust a few days after Mount Augustine erupted. It was as quiet as winter, but it made you feel uncomfortable and bleak when you looked outside.

The map of the world that my brother hung upside down on his bedroom wall, saying it is just arbitrary that we think of *north* as *up*.

.

The note I found on my mother's desk, written by an administrator for the British royal family, thanking her for her letter but assuring her that she was not the Duchess of Kent.

Once I caught a high fever and spent a day talking to the walls, which bowed outward from the corners of the room.

A lichen-covered human skull lying in a weathered coffin on an expanse of tundra, pushed up out of the frozen ground.

The balls of aluminum foil that my mother wadded onto the ends of our television antennae to protect us from radiation. That she would decide that foil could solve the problem, but not, say, rubber or Styrofoam.

The fancy plate of Asian glass noodles that my brother ordered at a restaurant in Hawaii. When it came, my mother said it looked like worms and wouldn't let him eat it. They argued about it for ten minutes before she made the waiter take the noodles back.

The crowd watching a parade that you are in. As you walk along, it feels like they're the parade.

A homeless man in Santa Fe who had a rat he had trained to lie on top of a cat, which curled up on top of a dog. They would remain that way for hours. The man said he was spreading the message of world peace.

For a while my mother wore bandannas over her face, bandit-style, every time she was in the kitchen. The practice developed to include a second bandanna over her forehead, so only her eyes were visible through the gap in the fabric.

That some questions in this world come with answers, and some do not.

The glowing end of a cigarette thrown from the window of a car in front of you at night, so that the orange light bounces on the pavement a few times.

The bullet I found one morning in Santa Fe, the metal all crumpled and unrecognizable, after it burst through my room-mate's window and then the Sheetrock wall of my closet while we slept, landing on the floor beside my bed.

My dog, stuck in a tree.

The miniature rubber bands my mother stretched across her teeth for months, as homemade orthodontic appliances. She refused to go to a dentist, and I winced somewhere inside every time she smiled.

When a forest fire fills the air with smoke, and the sun glows large and red and quivers like the end of the world.

The swath of burn-scarred tissue on my husband's shoulder, the size of my hand. I have never looked at it closely because it is too painful to take in all the details of such an injury to someone I love.

The months when my mother didn't seem to eat anything at all except cheddar cheese and green onions. She would stand

A Shapeless Thief

MY MOTHER KNOWS THE EARTH'S SURFACE IS COMPOSED OF tectonic plates, and that these plates move hundreds of miles with ease. They arrange and rearrange themselves, very quickly sometimes, creating natural phenomena when they shift. There is one place, the Shear, where the plates have fallen away, leaving a bare, scraped expanse extending for hundreds of miles. In another place, near Monterey, California, a plate dropping into the ocean has created a series of horizontal shelves at the continent's underwater edge. On one of these, she says, a city thrives beneath the waves.

Sometimes plates duplicate themselves or multiply, resulting in two or more that are nearly identical and seem to contain the same location. For this reason, she says, it's important to pay attention to details when you travel, to make sure you stay on the right plate—in the correct Roswell; in the Anchorage where you grew up. Each Roswell, each Anchorage, is a distinct colony. And if you accidentally end up on the wrong plate, you won't find the people you know, because they're not there. This is why flying is tricky. You go up in the air, and when you come down there's no real way of knowing if you've landed on the right plate or another by the same name. You fly to Santa Fe to see your sister, but when you go looking for her, you may not be able to find her.

So check the sky. See if it looks different today. Strange. See if it looks like a different sky than the sky you remember seeing over Santa Fe. And if you go to your sister's house and she's not there, look at the pillows. They might be the wrong color. These are the little things that help us know where we are.

In bits and pieces over many years, my mother has described to me this earth, the one she inhabits, expansively elaborating on the details of plates and colonies, as well as what she calls the Assay, a natural force that continually sorts us according to where we belong. It's more than a single fantasy. It's a whole system of rules and perceptions that together constitute an alternate world—a foundational delusion that emerged slowly in her mind when I was in high school and developed into a full-scale paracosm by the time I finished college.

I've been told that when I was very young and my mother was still sane, she sometimes spoke of the universe as existing in two streams. First Stream was our tangible, everyday reality. Second Stream was a separate, inner place, the realm of the imagination and spirit. Then the boundary between realities became so porous that she lost track of their differences. Metaphor entangled physical fact. The two streams ran together.

Now she doesn't bother to explain much, because she knows I understand the basics. She'll bring up the topic only if there are new developments, usually as a prelude to offering important advice: "Stay away from California for a little while." Or "Make sure you have plenty of gas!" This isn't overprotectiveness on her part; it's reasonable concern. Her world is one that is capable of shifting beneath her feet. The houses she has lived in, the cities they were built in, the very rock they stand on—all can be torn out from under her.

This may explain why, for a long time, she moved regularly through several states, never living in the same place for longer than a year but instead looping back to visit the same spots again and again. She never flew. Instead she'd take the train from New Mexico to Monterey. She'd work her way by bus up to Bellingham, and maybe take the ferry into Southeast Alaska, to Sitka or Juneau, sleeping in hostels and befriending the twenty-somethings she met there. Sometimes she would give me a name and a number. "Hang on to that," she'd say. "If you find yourself in a bad situation, this is someone you can contact for help." Or "Remember this name. If you meet someone by this name, you could take her home and give her a place to sleep for the night. She might become your roommate!"

My mother's travel habit began in the grip of her descent into psychosis three decades ago, when she was nearly forty and I was ten. She spun into a six-month round-the-world romp, jetting from Hawaii to North Africa to Australia, and then returned periodically to many of those places over the next several years. This was paid for by inherited money and fueled by a belief that someone was after her, and it may have started because my grandparents were trying to have her hospitalized. After a few months in and out of a clinic in Alaska, she went along with their plan to try one in Dallas. There the effort reached an unexpected climax when she bolted across a parking lot, jumped into a cab, and disappeared into the night. She resurfaced with a phone call, two weeks later, from the other side of the world.

I was offered few explanations for my mother's behavior, beyond being told by my father that she was "ill" and it was not her fault. At some point the word *schizophrenia* reached my ears, but it meant little to me. In place of understanding, I took hold of the tokens of her travels, as if they were crumbs I could follow to this new place inside her. Whenever she returned from a trip, she would bring back wonders for my sisters and brother and me to pore over—embroidered housedress-like garments from Algiers, all kinds of currencies. The Australian coins were our favorites: kangaroo, platypus. Once, my older sister, Alicia, organized the coins into a booklet and labeled them. Although we were savvy enough to sort out the sources of the various European currencies, there were a number whose origins we couldn't decipher from the script. Alicia labeled those "Arabic Nation." We had asked our mother, but she didn't know. She had gone missing in more ways than one.

To this day, my mother has never accepted the idea that she has a mental illness, and as far as I know she has never willingly taken medication for it. She has never been officially diagnosed with schizophrenia either, but she knows this is what people say about her. At least two doctors have said they believe she has some form of it. "Schizophrenic tendencies," one suggested. "Schizoaffective disorder," suspected another, naming the illness that includes symptoms of both schizophrenia and bipolar disorder. And it runs in our family—my brother began to show similar symptoms in his twenties and eventually received a schizophrenia diagnosis. (He, too, resisted the idea that he had an illness and refused treatment for years.) But official diagnosis for my mother would require a doctor's confirmation that her symptoms have lasted longer than one month, and none have connected with her meaningfully enough to make such an assessment. For nearly a quarter century, she wouldn't allow any doctor to examine her at all.

My sisters and I, on the other hand, have observed that her symptoms have lasted for more than thirty years.

Even when I was a child, the word *schizophrenia* struck me with its frightening poetry. Its exotic and convoluted array of letters captured the sense I had of the illness—confusing and bizarre, mysterious, infamously inscrutable. During the first few years of my mother's illness, I witnessed what I can only describe as a disintegration. Once a beautiful woman leading a healthy, engaged life, she transformed into a mistrustful recluse who subsisted on cigarettes and screwdrivers while her teeth rotted away. For a while she nearly imprisoned us in our own house, barring the door with heavy pieces of furniture and having lengths of wood fit to the windows so they could not be slid open. She was so afraid of assassins that her fear seeped into me too. I did as she asked for a long time. After a while, though, I rebelled, and eventually I just gave up, choosing instead to detach myself by playing video games all afternoon while she snacked on bowls of cake batter or simply sat very still for hours on end.

I rarely found words for what I saw my mother do, what I heard her say, so her illness seemed to always live in the shadows. In the closet, under the bed. As a child I felt schizophrenia to be a dark, shapeless thief. What other image fit what I had seen? How does a child articulate the absence of what is necessary? The absence of sanity. The absence of the mother I had known. To my eye it appeared, more than anything, that she had been stolen.

Now, grown and far more educated, I often feel nearly the same. Schizophrenia still defies the most fundamental question about it: What *is* it? I can tell you it is a brain disorder that causes distortions in perception, thought, and emotion. I can explain that it arises by way of chemical and physical processes inside the brain. But if I reach much further, I soon arrive at the edge of human knowledge. We have not yet fully grasped how the brain creates perception, thought, and emotion to begin with, let alone such spectacular distortions. One important review compared contemporary researchers' various hypotheses to the parable of the blind men and the elephant: Each, when asked what an elephant looked like, felt a different part of the beast and described it. One, feeling its trunk, said it was shaped like a snake. Another, feeling a leg, proclaimed that it was shaped like a tree . . .

Schizophrenia is not a disease as the term is generally understood, but rather a syndrome—a constellation of symptoms that tend to occur together and tend to be causally linked. Psychiatrists still debate, in fact, whether schizophrenia is a single disorder or a conglomeration of separate disorders arising from disparate causes. Sometimes referred to as the "schizophrenia spectrum," the condition as envisioned by the latest diagnostic guidelines is more like a matrix of symptoms that gradually fade into normalcy. This is why the presence of "significant social and occupational dysfunction" is crucial for doctors to consider—though that, too, occurs on a spectrum. The line between mental health and mental illness, though sometimes a practical necessity, isn't really a line so much as an open plain.

Officially, schizophrenia is categorized as a "psychotic disorder," and of all its symptoms, the most famous are features of psychosis, the state in which a person's thoughts and perceptions are so distorted that she effectively inhabits a separate reality. Psychosis includes hallucinations, delusions, and profound mental disorganization, as well as a more fundamental shift in the way the world seems and feels—and all of this interacts with personality and memory. My mother's most visible sign of illness, her delusional thinking, is at this point so deeply intertwined with her emotional life that it is often hard for me to know which of her actions stem from delusions and which do not.

The inherited wealth that paid for my mother's globe-trotting is now long gone. A dozen years ago or so, needing an allowance from my grandmother, she returned to the epicenter of her family—New Mexico—and stayed nearby for several years, hopping regularly between Roswell, Santa Fe, Denver, and Tucson, places where most of her six brothers and sisters and various other relatives lived. This was for her a fairly circumscribed and blessedly consistent movement pattern, although she still ranged farther from time to time.

In my early thirties, I lived in Santa Fe for several years while she was also in the state, so during that time I could see her regularly. She also called often, which was important to me, since she had no telephone for most of that time and I couldn't call her. She was too paranoid to keep a phone of her own, but would use pay phones and relatives' phones. She just wouldn't leave a message, ever, and while on the phone she wouldn't refer to people she knew by name, and if you lingered without speaking for more than a couple of beats, she'd hang up on you. If behind this paranoia there was a delusion, however—some false, unshakable belief that would make sense of it—she never explained it to me.

A new pattern emerged when I moved to New York and she stopped calling me. Before moving, I reiterated several times that I wanted her to call me regularly, but she skirted the issue, and it was only after I left that I realized there was something in her mind getting in the way.

When I visited Santa Fe a few months later, I tried again, although I didn't think it would make a difference. "Mom," I said, "*call* me."

"Oh, well, you're over there now," she said. "So far away! I think it's better to—to stay close."

"Yeah, but, why does that matter? It's a phone."

"Hmmm. I try to call Sadie," she said, referring to my younger sister, who lived in Santa Fe too. "I've been trying to call Sadie! She never answers."

"Sadie has to turn her phone off when she's at work. So call *me*."

"Well. I think I'm just going to stay focused on what's nearby. I just think that's a good idea right now."

Our conversations are riddled with these inexplicable refusals—inflexible positions she won't relinquish and won't, or can't, explain. They emerge from nowhere and stick like cement. A decade before, when I was in graduate school in New Hampshire, she called me often. But in New York it was as if I had fallen off the edge of the world. Eventually she moved back to Alaska and got a phone again. Now I can call her, and she's delighted when I do, but she still won't call me herself.

Certain places, it seems, must be avoided. When Alicia got married in Bozeman, Montana, our mother missed the wedding. I cajoled and then harassed her about it as the date approached, but she was evasive. Every time I brought it up, she shifted the focus to the lovely wedding gift she had bought.

At first I thought she didn't like the idea of attending a crowded event, so I tried bargaining. "You don't have to go to the reception," I told her. "You can just go to the ceremony." When that failed, I went all the way. "You don't even have to go to the ceremony," I said. "You can just see Alicia before-hand, on that day. Or the day before."

I got nowhere. She wouldn't relent and wouldn't say why. I have since racked my brain trying to understand what it is about Bozeman. If it is Bozeman at all. But her whole world is a cipher, and in it there are codes I can't break.

In her youth my mother was one of those people who seemed to catch everyone's eye. "Like a sprite," my aunts say. "Like an elf." Petite and pale, with a heart-shaped face and a delicate smile, she was beautiful and alluring and had a distinctive, distant charm. Now in her seventies, thick around the middle with her once dark hair a peppery gray, she still seems some-how like a pixie. Her eyes dart about and her hands flit with precision as she speaks. When quiet, she turns inward, and it is almost as if I am watching her curl her head under a wing. She isn't beautiful anymore. Jowls hang low on her face, and when she smiles she reveals teeth weathered and crooked from malnutrition and neglect. But her blue eyes seem to have inten-sified in color, and her bony fingers are as articulate as ever.

These days, my mother has a very clear sense of what kind of information upsets others—things "people don't like to hear about." So she has been in the habit, for decades, of reserving the discussion of such topics for my sisters and me.

"Marin, I'm glad you're here, because there are some important things I need to tell you about," she said once, peering at me with wide eyes and her hands clasped politely in her lap. "I've learned about a few things that I think you might want to do. I have found out—I've found out that now is a good time to move to Pluto."

Despite her refusal to accept her illness, she knows that the world reaches her in a different form than it reaches others, and I am almost certain she knows that something about this cripples her. But she still fights for the validity of her thoughts, as anyone else would.

"Pluto?" I asked. "Like, the planet?"

"There are some exciting developments happening there right now, and you can buy a home at a good price. Right now, before it really catches on. They're setting up a colony there. Homes for young people, and you're at the age that you could go there and really get started on your life."

"Mom," I said, "I have a life."

"Oh, but this is such a great opportunity! It's so afford-able! You could really find a nice house there and have a nice place to live."

There is no point in arguing with delusions, but I also hate to play along with them. Usually I engage just a little, to show I care. This time I offered something like "So, how do you know they're colonizing Pluto?" But I'm not very good at hiding my impatience.

"I've seen it! I've seen—I know this, Marin. I've—I under-stand this." She paused, her eyes searching. I could practically see the wheels turning as she sorted through her mind looking for a response solid enough that I wouldn't silently reject it. As much as she's shared the material of her delusions with me, she almost never lets slip anything about where they come from or how they're formed. And she knows I'm a skeptical listener.

"Such a beautiful place! Do you know the oceans there have waves that are capped with fire? Can you imagine? Fire-capped waves?"

"That's a beautiful image," I said, genuinely, picturing it. "It kind of takes your breath away."

"Yes, it does, doesn't it? And there are all these condos for sale there now! You might want to do that!"

"Mom," I said gently, "I just really want to be here right now, okay?"

"Well, think about it and see if you don't change your mind. Also, there's something else I want to explain to you too. Your uncle Robert has been staying in the condo in Santa Fe, and I want you to know that the condo belongs to me. It's mine, and he—*somebody*—took it away from me. Now, while I don't have any home at all, he goes and stays in that place and acts like it belongs to him."

I was annoyed now, inevitably, though I felt for her, that she no longer owned a place of her own. I rubbed my forehead and said something like "As far as I know, the condo has always been Robert's." I said it wearily, not to convince her, but just because it was a reasonable response that was neither condescending nor untrue. The condo did belong to Robert, but I qualified the statement to acknowledge that I had never actually seen the deed.

"Well, it wasn't always his," she countered. "He went and got the papers from where they were filed, and the people at City Hall didn't notice, and now he's told everyone it's his, and there are no papers, so everybody thinks it *is* his. But maybe one of these days, Marin—this is why I'm telling you this—those papers might turn up. So if you see, at some point, some papers that look like they have to do with a house, if you find them lying around somewhere, I want you to take them and keep them someplace safe. Because then I might be able to get my house back."

"I don't think they would leave those kinds of papers just lying around," I said.

"Well, you never know. You never know!"

Sometimes I just stare at her and remind myself that she's on her own trip and it's not my job to fix the unfixable. But she tends to persist, and did, until I said something like "If I *happen* to come across some papers that look like the deed to Robert's condo, I'll do that."

"Good," she said. "Now, what are you up to today?"

Other times, though, her voice might turn sad. As in dreams, much of the symbolism in her delusions hints at her own feelings about her life as she struggles to understand it. But this is a dream she can't wake up from.

"All these homes I've had, that people have taken away from me!" she once said plaintively. She lifted her chin and gazed into the distance with innocent eyes. "It's almost too much for a person."

And that was too much for *me*. Although I know that nobody has ever taken a home from her or even claimed any property that was rightly hers, I wanted to tell her I wouldn't let anything bad happen to her. But I could never say that, really. I've never been able to protect her from anything.

For nearly two decades, since my mother sold the two-bedroom house in Santa Fe that she had bought when I was in college, she has been wondering how she lost her home. She keeps searching for a place where she can live and be safe for the rest of her life. But she's too erratic and irrational. She has spent all the money that bought her former houses—a trust fund from my once wealthy grandfather, a divorce settlement, her own sporadic earnings from jobs as a gift store cashier or a cafeteria server. Since then, living on Social Security and an allowance from the family, she has gone through a string of small apartments, one after another, rarely committing to a lease longer than six months.

To explain this, I have only a theory, based on things she has described over the years: Each time she arrives at a place, it is new, unsignified, a clean slate. Then her visions and voices, loaded with emotional import, begin interacting with that physical environment, and slowly, over the course of months, meanings accrue. All the powers of the universe work their way into the smallest details. *Here is where a bright light visited me one night. I stayed quiet for it and watched.* Around the time her psychosis set in, she became devoutly Christian, more so than anyone else in her Lutheran-Episcopalian family, and she now often interprets errant perceptions as miracles. But other times, the details of her encounters turn ominous or antagonistic. *Someone has been burying horses in the backyard. I've seen the teeth coming up out of the ground!* Eventually, every detail of the place seethes and echoes so resoundingly with the influence of powers only she can see—everything pointing back to her, for her, about her—that the only way to keep it under control is to flee.

This is, I think, why she couldn't remain at her mother's house in Roswell, her hometown, despite being welcome to live there for free. The dozens of paintings on my grandmother's walls made her uncomfortable. She started moving things around, hiding things. It baffled my aunts and uncles and frustrated my grandmother. I could only glean what my mother wouldn't say outright: The paintings were looking at her, talking to her, and when they upset or frightened her too much, she had to escape them. She put them away in corners to sap them of their power, and when my aunts and uncles tried to convince or force her to stop doing this, she moved out. Then she started renting apartments for a few months or a year, bought a white comforter, and kept nothing on the walls but a small cross and an image of whatever saint had recently caught her attention.

I think if she had a house of her own, she might still leave it periodically for months at a time. But she wants that house, her house. She wants to see the return of at least one of the many homes she has lost in her lifetime, which she believes were stolen. And the weird truth is that, in a way, they *were* stolen. Schizophrenia stole them, by taking away her capacity for long-term planning and remembering. The ability to keep track of time is a prerequisite for virtually everything a person can have or do in life. In the timeline of the universe, my mother lives in a bubble that disintegrates into chaos two weeks in either direction. That's about the extent to which she can pin reality down well enough to at least manage her life within it. Beyond that it becomes too warped to be of use.

She can manage a weekly budget but not a yearly budget. She can sublet a room but gets paranoid about the paperwork required to qualify for low-income housing. She can do fairly complex tasks like shopping, cooking, or balancing a checkbook, but has always had trouble maintaining the relationships required to keep a job. Momentary concerns overwhelm the bigger picture, which dissipates into mist.

Trying to help my mother is a frustrating and usually futile effort. She won't often accept help, preferring, she says, to take care of things herself. The harder we push, the more she resists. I try to be as cooperative as possible, hoping she'll go along with my plans if I act optimistic. But mostly, my hands are tied. Over the years, we in her family have sometimes tried to maneuver around her to get her finances under control, but we couldn't do much without her permission. No one could have forcefully intervened. She functions far too well to be declared incompetent. This is how it happened that she squandered all she had, spending more to live than she could earn, buying and selling a long series of houses, condos, apartments, and cars, each time losing money on the deal until she had nothing left.

When people first meet my mother, she peers up at them expectantly, immediately asks how their day has been, and often says something disarmingly cute. She's fond of giving gifts, doling them out almost as offerings to the gods: a coupon for a latte at Starbucks, a brochure for a luxury cruise in the Caribbean. "Look at this," she'll say, holding up the photo of a jewel-blue seascape. "You may be interested in doing something like this in the future. Maybe this will give you ideas."

She may or may not decide to say something risky. And if she does, it may or may not be apparent that it's a delusion. Often it's necessary to know the people she mentions in order to know whether what she's saying is true. Relating to my mother involves a delicate interplay between realities, one that few people are prepared to learn. My role is to be her translator. When she speaks to friends of mine, I try to stand slightly behind her so I can signal—a sharp nod or a quick shake of the head—to indicate whether they should interpret a given story as fact or fantasy.

When my mother first met my husband, Will (then a new boyfriend), in a Santa Fe bookstore, she pulled a book on Italian cooking off the nearest shelf and asked if he liked Italian food. She concentrated hard for a moment, and as she continued I could see her working her way toward a thought. It was clear from her manner that she was seeking, not scheming— listening, perhaps, to the ruler of her secret world. Then she announced that my dad was a friend of the book's celebrity-chef author, Giada De Laurentiis. Only after we left could I tell Will that my dad had never met Giada De Laurentiis—

though he does make great Italian food. The delusion apparently sprang up as my mother was speaking.

Other things my father has done, according to my mother, include being swept away in a tsunami in Hawaii in the mid-eighties. As she tells it, he drowned, and in the confusion, another man appeared and took his place. This man was very helpful and began taking care of us, and after a while nobody noticed anymore that he wasn't our real dad. He let everyone call him by our dad's name, and for a while my mother believed that he was the real thing. But a few years later she caught on, and when I was about twelve she explained to me that the man I called Dad was not actually my father but a replacement. "I call him Mr. Ree," she said. I didn't catch the significance of the name until Alicia sardonically spelled it out for me: "Myster-ry."

As the rest of us experienced it, my mother divorced my father in 1984, when I was ten, in a period of sustained and probably paranoia-based rage, after nearly a dozen years of marriage and the birth of four children. Dad, still largely in denial of her descent into psychosis, bought and moved into the house next door, and we settled into a joint custody arrangement just as the true extent of her illness became clear. Years later, when I asked him why he hadn't fought for sole custody, he said, "I just couldn't do that to your mother." For the rest of my childhood, my dad was in that same house and my mother stayed within the neighborhood. We moved back and forth between the two houses about once a week.

For years my mother would refer to my dad only as Ree. "How is Ree?" she would say when I was at her house. "Are things okay over there at his house?"

At some point in my teens, I dryly asked her if it bothered her that her children were being raised by a stranger.

"Well," she said, "he seems to be a nice enough man and he has really, truly accepted this work of taking care of you kids. So I guess it's worked out okay."

Her mind is forever another country, a long-lost homeland that only she has seen. And I am her bridge, even when I can't see one side from the other.

Nowadays my mother's delusions fade in and out, and with these shifts her memory changes. Sometimes she still calls my dad Ree, and other times by his real name. It was not long after their divorce that he first became Mr. Ree—not long after he, in a last-ditch effort to get help for her, had her briefly committed at the state psychiatric hospital. During the next two or three years, her rage and paranoia toward him were so thick that she couldn't speak to him without shouting, and for a while she wouldn't allow him to see her face. She kept her head shrouded in a scarf when she drove up his driveway to drop us off. Now, when her stolen-house delusions turn toward the cabin he owns and when she tells me why it rightfully belongs to her, he is Ree. But when, maybe, she hasn't thought about him for a while and isn't upset about anything relating to him, Ree slips away and he is himself once again.

The hardest losses for me to witness are this kind—not of home or fortune but of the relationships her illness has made so difficult. Or impossible, as with anyone she comes to fear or mistrust through her paranoid beliefs. I know she feels these losses as much as any. The inevitable by-product is her own loneliness.

Even for my sisters and me, loving our mother is never simple. My younger sister, Adrienne, is an ongoing point of confusion, because she usually goes by her nickname, Sadie. My mother seems to assume that Adrienne and Sadie are different people, but she doesn't take issue with the double identity. I didn't even realize that this was the case until one of my aunts mentioned a conversation she had with my mother while Adrienne was traveling in Asia.

"Is Adrienne still in India?" my aunt asked.

"Yes," my mother answered, "and I think Sadie is too."

For a few years she also thought there were two of Alicia. I may be the only one who remains singular, and I admit this has always been a little bit of a relief for me—although I know my doppelgänger could emerge at any time.

"Mom," I once asked her, "don't you think it's strange that I'm the only one there has never been two of?"

"Oh, I know!" she said. "Isn't that remarkable? It's just amazing how things can happen sometimes. Everyone but you!"

For many years, my mother was sure that my brother had, like my father, been swept away in a tidal wave in Hawaii and that this little boy who called her Mom was another child. This boy, this false Tom, was just as sweet as her Tom, however, so she embraced him as her own. But she worried that the real Tom was still out there, lost and alone. She only hoped someone kind and loving had taken him in.

She has found lost children everywhere she's gone. They're always young people, often travelers, and when she speaks of them to me, it is to ask for my help in keeping an eye out in case they might need shelter or a surrogate family. "You can adopt each other!" she says sometimes. One of her more elaborate delusions involves an actual organization, the Arc of Anchorage, which in reality provides support for people with disabilities but which she says offers the service of facilitating the process by which people can adopt each other. Because there are so many of these orphans wandering around, she explained to me, somebody decided to help them take care of each other.

When my brother was still alive, she often suggested that I adopt him. She knew, because I told her, that he was in Anchorage but that on any given day I didn't know where he was. I didn't know what she made of that. She hadn't seen him for several years. But I could tell that she knew, from her own observations and intuition, that her son was struggling and isolated.

"Any news from up north?" she asked me every time we talked. This was her way of saying, "Have you heard from your brother?"

"Not lately," I almost always answered.

"Why don't you give the house a call?" she suggested next.

"You mean Dad's house?"

"Yes."

"I can't reach Tom by calling Dad's house," I said. "He doesn't like to go to Dad's house." For a long time I used this reply to evade what I never had the heart, or the guts, to explain. But when Adrienne told me she had already tried to explain that Tom was mentally ill, with unclear results, I thought I should give it a try too. When I visited Santa Fe a few months later, my mother asked for news from Alaska. I looked at her squarely. "I can't call Tom because I don't know where he is," I said. I took a breath. "He's homeless. He lives on the street."

She looked down, her face furrowed in annoyance, and began picking a cuticle.

"Tom has schizophrenia, Mom," I said.

"Oh, don't say that!" she said, pulling her hands back close to her body, still looking down and picking at her fingers.

"That's why I can't call him." She wouldn't look at me.

"Come on, now, Marin! Let's not talk about that today."

My words sounded cruel in my ears as they grated across her. But I hate to hide the truth from her. Her mind does that so brutally well already.

"Tom is going to deal with his life," she said sternly, "the way he decides to. Now let's not talk about this." I realized she had already thought this through. And she got it right— for years my brother refused help from anyone, even help to get off the street. She understood, perhaps better than anyone, that his struggles were ultimately his to overcome.

The balm for these rough times comes in the small moments, the easy ones. Moments when nothing can be gained or lost, when one of us notices something lovely in the world: She sees a bird outside the window and remarks at the brilliance of its red wing. She bends to pet my dog and comments on how daintily she lifts her paw. For all the confusion and fear induced by her ever-reconfiguring world, it also grants her the full richness of its magic.

Driving down the road in Santa Fe one spring morning, when a gust of wind picked up a spray of fallen pink petals and swirled them over the road in front of my car, I wished she were there to see it. I knew she would feel its beauty and for a moment be filled by it. I miss her whenever I have these moments alone. One day in Central Park, I walked past a shadowy grove of leafless trees after a morning rain had left their branches laden with drops of water, clinging so densely that they seemed like pearls strung along the undersides of the limbs. "Mom!" I wanted to say. "Look at the droplets of water shining on the trees!"

"Oh!" she would reply, "isn't that lovely!" Her voice would be high, captivated. She would pause. Her bubble in space-time would encompass us both, and for a moment I would feel as if the entire world began and ended there.

Chokecherries

IN THE EARLY YEARS, WHEN MY MOTHER WAS STILL SANE, she cut lengths of pussy willow branches at Easter and arranged them in vases. Not yet budded, they came laden with soft silver pods like rabbits' feet. She took colored powders and dusted the furry pods. Pale yellow, pink, lavender, blue.

She told my father, "They're trying to kill us." She said, "They're coming after us." She said, "They are a band of assassins hired by the CIA to kill the families of ex–Green Berets." He said to her, "That doesn't make any god damn sense."

Reality is slippery. If someone tells you something often enough for long enough, regardless of whether it's true, you begin to believe it. Or at least you might begin to doubt your own perceptions, think, *Maybe she knows something I don't know. Maybe I'm missing something. Maybe there's something here that I don't understand.*

Neuroscientists, when asked to define "the mind," suggest that it is a process—an emergent property that arises from the brain and regulates its flow of energy and information. Some also say that the mind is not strictly an embodied process but rather a relational one, emerging not only from the brain but also from interactions with other minds.

At night, my father's voice came from the living room up the stairwell, loud, rising over my mother's as he told her: "No, no, no." I fell asleep to the muffled sound of shouts. It was a strange silence when she kicked him out and he moved into his own place down the street, so that her house was still as I drifted off.

Her delusions were astonishing. That assassins had implanted a radio transmitter in her brain. That they had left a wad of gum on the carpet or dropped a toothpick in line behind her at the grocery store, as death threats. She blocked the door with furniture every night.

She took my sisters and brother and me to hotels when she thought they were watching us. We slept there on school nights, displaced, broken from our routine as she remade our world. When we stayed home she paced in the darkness, peering into our bedrooms to check on us. In the car, she told us to duck and hide behind the seats. At first we went along with it, wanting to believe her.

It occurs to me that mental illness and madness are not the same thing. Mental illness is a set of brain malfunctions with psychological effects, like paranoia, delusions, insomnia. Madness is a state of incoherence—paradoxical, or nonsensical, or untenable. Madness sometimes arises from mental illness, but it may arise in other ways as well. This distinction is important because mental illness is not contagious, but madness often is.

. . .

In 1989, computer science student Mark Humphrys developed an artificial intelligence program, called MGonz, that was designed to mimic human conversation. When MGonz was ready, Humphrys posted it online and left for the day. While he was gone, a user with the screen name Someone sent Humphrys's account the salutation "finger," an early command used to make contact with remote users. MGonz replied, "Cut this cryptic shit speak in full sentences." Someone was apparently insulted. The two proceeded to argue, heatedly, for an hour and a half. The next day, Humphrys found the contents of the conversation log to be so profane that he wasn't sure he could publish his findings.

My mother hung baskets of flowers by the front door. She was fond of the drooping vines with red and purple blooms that looked like their name, bleeding hearts. The words for one thing became the words for another thing. Language stepped sideways, doubled, flipped. This idea intrigued me, even more so when I began to understand that she now spoke in code. "Don't go outside" meant "I've lost my mind."

After my parents' divorce, my mother would call and yell at my father over the phone, attacking him for things he hadn't done and hadn't said. If we were at his house, he refused to fight with her in front of us. "Okay," he would say into the receiver, his tone barely contained. "I gotta go now. Bye.

Goodbye." He told us he was going to be rational with her even when she was irrational.

Folie à deux: a psychiatric syndrome in which a delusional belief is transmitted from one individual to another living in close proximity. Typically, both people involved have a delusional disorder, but the delusion is generated inside only one mind and then spreads and takes root in the other. The term translates as "madness shared by two." Recognized as a phenomenon in scientific literature since the nineteenth century, folie à deux has confounded doctors for two centuries, because it is not compatible with the Western concept of the mind as separate and distinct to an individual brain.

We were kids. We forgot appointments. We forgot to put the milk away. We forgot our shoes at our mother's house. My father told us, "You forgot because you don't care. You don't care, that's why." He said it to us over and over, a chant, a prayer. "You think that's what I'm here for. You think I'm here to clean up your messes. Because you don't give a god damn." If I said to him that I did care, that I always cared, he told me, "No, you don't. You don't care."

Yarrow filled the edges of the front garden, sprouting clusters of tiny white flowers that were impossible to pluck. The thick, stringy stem was too strong. I tried twisting and pinching, but nothing worked. I yanked until the entire two-foot stalk, roots and all, gave way.

Researchers who study artificial intelligence categorize verbal abuse, as well as typical argumentative posturing, as modes of communicating that are "stateless." Stateless conversations proceed only from the last thing the last speaker said. The progress of a stateless conversation is detached from all context. This was how MGonz succeeded in tricking Someone into believing it was human. When MGonz didn't know what to say next, it masked its limitations by falling back on off-topic put-downs like "You are obviously an asshole."

My mother cut a square out of the living room carpet, one foot by one foot, saying it had a bad smell. She would sit for hours, staring at the space in front of her, silent, still, a ghost in her own life. When she spoke, her words were charged, full, irrelevant. In the kitchen, we foraged for breakfast.

According to postmodern theorists, every story that is told masks the absence of every other story that could have been told in its place. What is absent matters as much as what is present. When my father yelled about our failures, he left no room for other things we might have communicated. We didn't talk about life at our mother's house. We didn't say what frightened us, or why. We didn't risk appearing vulnerable. We didn't ask for help understanding the things that confounded us, like sanity and insanity. So our own lives became unreal, even as they overwhelmed us.

In the front yard grew a massive chokecherry tree. Chokecherries were beguiling blue-black balls that, when squeezed, bled purple juice. I tasted one once, feeling the burst of liquid so bitter it felt dry, stripping my mouth of its moisture as it spread across my tongue to the back of my throat, closing it up. For a moment I could not breathe, swallow, speak.

Once, when I skinned my knee, my father said, "I don't do sympathy. You can go to your mother for that." He said, "Your mother's great at that kind of thing." This was long after an opaque and distant stillness had overtaken her. I had by this time forgotten that she had ever been great at that kind of thing. I looked at him and wondered what he was talking about.

. . .

Recent case studies involving folie à deux report that a delusion, generated internally by the dominant person in a relationship, can then be picked up by the non-dominant person and believed with equal commitment and intensity. But folie à deux does not lead to a sense of togetherness against a common foe. A delusional state is too solipsistic to allow for that. Rather, each individual experiences the shared delusion as entirely his or her own, each feeling singularly trapped and isolated within it.

It only now strikes me as odd that my father refrained from yelling at our mother, for our sake, and then yelled at us when he was upset at her. He didn't see the contradiction here.

There were gooseberries. Pale green orbs with stripes a shade paler, and tufts of fiber at one end. Sour. They grew on the thorny bush in the backyard.

We think of talking as a means of connecting with others, but as MGonz and Someone revealed, stateless conversation does the opposite. Verbal abuse supersedes and prevents connection, and it sustains an ongoing lack of connection. Instead it creates an illusion of connection that masks its actual absence. In my father's house, the alienation was double, not just from each other but from the much larger questions that hung over us. Were we still a family? Would we turn out okay? Did we need him to be both a father and a mother? Could he rise to that challenge?

Rhubarb sprouted in a shady strip of garden running along the edge of the deck, casually tended by my mother. I've learned, from the NIH website, that rhubarb leaves contain oxalic acid and anthraquinone glycosides. If ingested, the leaves cause burning in the mouth and throat, nausea, vomiting, weakness, diarrhea, seizures, coma.

Sometimes, when little was at stake, sympathy flowed out of my father naturally. When I had the flu, he would walk softly into my room and whisper to me as he sat on the edge of my bed, fussing over my tissues and my glass of water and blankets. He did not blame me for the flu, didn't take it as my failure, or his own. No one was implicated.

Now I use language to nail things down. I prefer precise words. I like to say exactly what I mean. What I mean to ask: What is the mind? Where does it begin and end? What I mean to say: To answer these questions, the mind has only itself to turn to. What I mean to consider: Reality is an amalgam of perceptions and ideas whose validity is always being negotiated—and what we accept as real is what has been approved by consensus.

·

Even after going back through conversations with my father in my mind and pinpointing the moments in which he departed from logic, from the realities of me and him—when he abandoned the observable truth about me for some idea he had formed before I even emerged from the womb—I would still ask myself, *Is this somehow my doing? Is this somehow my fault?*

We gathered rhubarb stalks and munched on them raw. My mother told us not to eat the leaves. Only the stems were edible. The leaves, she said, were poison.

The Rumor[1]

I WAS MAYBE THIRTEEN WHEN WE HEARD THE RUMOR THAT twice a year, on the equinoxes, it is possible to balance an egg on its end. The story went that on those days the earth's gravitational pull is aligned just so, making it easy to keep the egg upright, whereas on most days this would be nearly impossible. It was said that this is especially true near the poles, and since we lived in Alaska, that put us in a good position to try it out. My dad was the kind of person who got excited about fun facts, so we pulled out a carton and each grabbed an egg. It was March, the first day of spring.[2]

---

1 Notes on Insanity and Forgetting

2 Those were the years when we lived half the time at our father's house and half the time with our mother—all but Alicia who lived always with our father, avoiding our mother and her madness. My father's approach to dealing with the fact of our mother's illness was to confront it when it posed a direct threat to us, and otherwise ignore it. Early on in her psychosis, he tried to clarify for us what exactly was happening, carefully explaining what it meant to have "schizophrenic tendencies." But he also decided that, when we were at his house, he would keep our minds off her problems by occupying us with other things.

firmation I've ever gotten. Once, wondering what the real explanation was, I hunted around online for a while, only to find the phenomenon consistently put down as a myth. Yes, the science geeks who conducted home experiments said, you *can* balance an egg on its end on the equinox—but that's just because you can do it on any day, if you really try. They even tested it at different latitudes, including in Alaska. I found no other conclusions.[6]

But no, I wanted to tell the egg experimenters. *It wasn't like that.* It was so *easy* to stand up the eggs on the equinox. *Not* like any other day. We'd pop one up in a couple of seconds. We got good at it. If you left it there undisturbed, it might stay standing for a week. But as the days passed, if it fell, it became notably more difficult to stand it back up. Until one day you stood there hunched over the countertop for half an hour and couldn't get the egg upright at all.[7]

I thought of our eggs when I read another woman's account of her mother's long psychotic episode during her teenage

---

6 What's most difficult now, when I look back on those years, is to realize what could have been changed for the better. There was no altering my mother's psychosis as long as she refused to take medication, and for years I found a degree of solace in the impossibility of helping her. But it's distressing to recall the way the illness was handled by my family. The breaking apart of lived reality and acknowledged reality. The new kind of madness this birthed.

7 I looked first to my father to confirm what I saw in my mother, and I didn't find it. Then in adulthood I asked aunts, uncles, grandparents about it. Some, in their retellings, erased whole decades of psychosis from the story. A few didn't seem to fully grasp the simple, raw fact that their sister was profoundly disabled. Who could I believe? Who was bullshitting? Who was forgetting? Either my siblings and I had always known much more about our mother's illness than anyone else in our family, or I'd had it wrong all along. *Was she really that delusional? Was it really that bad?*

years. I thought of our eggs when she admitted that afterward, for a while, she had actually succeeded in convincing herself that her mother's madness had never happened. I found myself frantic to prove that what I saw, what I did, was real.[8]

It happened. I swear it. I know it. It happened. I see them still, those eggs. White on the white Formica. Smooth and faintly stippled, reflecting the countertop's glow, soft in the pale light cast through the sliding doors. My brother is there, head down, the angles of his knuckles distinct as he maneuvers his egg, catches the sweet spot, pulls away. What was that? What was it? What?

---

8 Nowadays, when I'm on the phone with my mother and she's in a talkative mood, I compulsively type out her delusions: *They come through smiling and invade your home . . . and if you resist in any way, they just kill you . . . Poaching is killing!* Sometimes, looking later at the transcripts, I find myself floored. In all their pure verbatim glory, they still seem too extreme, too starkly impossible, to be what I actually heard. Without transcripts my memory tames them, rounds out the edges. Sometimes I wonder why I do it to myself, this transcribing. Why force myself to feel the full brunt of her insanity again and again? Maybe it is only in the truth of her illness, unabridged and uncensored, that I have been able to find some sanity of my own.

A World of Absolute Order

WHEN I FIRST BEGAN WATCHING SVETLANA BOGINSKAYA compete, she was not yet a legend in the sport of gymnastics, not well known outside the Soviet Union. She was still a surprise and I was barely a teenager. That was near the beginning of my own gymnastics career, which started several years after Svetlana's but to which I latched on quickly—having come to it, as it happened, by way of suddenly finding myself without a mother. The summer of the year my mother disappeared, my father had enrolled Adrienne and me in a beginner class to give us something to do while he was at work. So as I zipped through the list of skills to learn, mastering them in rapid succession, I was also contending with the fact that my mother had been altered, profoundly, by the mental illness that would cripple her for the rest of her life.

It is not coincidence that gymnastics became my escape from my family's predicament, and it is not coincidence that I found Svetlana. My first years as a gymnast were years of watching my mother deteriorate, both as a parent and as a person—years in which I was discovering all the various and contradictory ways that I had lost her. Between the ages of twelve and eighteen, I never spent longer than two weeks away from a gym.

What you noticed first about Svetlana when she stepped up to an apparatus was the length of her limbs. At nearly five feet, four inches, she was one of the tallest elite gymnasts in the world. This made the sport more challenging for her but more obviously had the effect of exaggerating her personal elegance, especially when she was in the air. When she began to move, those long lines took over, emphasizing the fluidity of her turns and accentuating her acrobatics so that in simple tumbling moves she seemed to hang in space for a beat or two.

She was known, too, as an exceptional twister. This became widely visible at the 1988 Olympics, in the floor routine that won her a silver medal and helped the USSR earn a team gold: Her first tumbling pass was a simple full-in-back-out—two tucked backflips in the air with a twist in the first one. Her second pass was a two-part sequence in which a laid-out front flip with one and a half twists led into a double-twisting layout—a laid-out backflip with two full twists. A grand total of four and a half twists. When she drove these moves home, it was viscerally gratifying to hear the slam of her feet on the floor. Flight, so many spins in the air that a novice viewer couldn't keep track, then *bam!* Glue.

The landings. The full length of Svetlana's body furled when she landed, almost like she was taking a bow. She bent much more deeply than most gymnasts do, particularly when vaulting or dismounting. Then, after that hammer-like motion nailed her feet to the floor, she arose from that low posture as if her spine were being unrolled by a dowel—one vertebra at a time. It was a subtle but remarkable habit that lingered in a viewer's mind. Certainty, then a measure of grace.

Even in the earliest footage of Svetlana in competition—at the 1985 Junior Cup, when she was only twelve years old and not yet at her full adult height—she was already displaying the trademarks of her gymnastics style. She went on to win two team championships at the Olympics, in 1988 and 1992. All told, she took home five Olympic medals, three of them gold. In her eleven years competing at the international level, she also won a World Championship all-around title, collected various wins at World Cups and European Championships, and twice earned a perfect ten in the floor exercise. But she was distinct among champions—famous less for winning than for winning in a particular way. Exactly what way, however, is harder to articulate.

I don't follow gymnastics anymore. The sport has changed so much since I quit competing twenty-odd years ago that I don't recognize many of the moves and am easily confused by the new elite scoring system. But Svetlana has stayed with me, clung to me, so that even now I can't bring myself to refer to her by her last name. Young girls never know their idols that way.

What I recall is that in competition, she held a cool but potent gaze that revealed nothing and everything. She rarely smiled, but never came off as fierce. Serious. She was always serious. She had an air of inaccessibility. That was part of her allure. Her eyes—small, deep, almond-shaped, fully lined with black kohl—seemed dark although they were pale blue. She was beautiful, with a small nose and pert lips, and an announcer once noted her striking resemblance to the actress Rebecca De Mornay. When I watch her now I think of Russian ballet, of Tchaikovsky, as many Americans must have in 1988, upon seeing Soviet gymnasts again after Cold War boycotts had kept them out of our living rooms for more than a decade. Soviet gymnasts were noticeably more graceful than our powerhouse American competitors, and they tended to have a quiet composure rarely seen here. We were the land of Mary Lou's mega-grin. With Svetlana, you could never tell if she was happy or if she was sad.

It helped, too, that Svetlana was a master of the perfectly straight line—an element fundamental to the sport, informing nearly every move in every event. Given this and her long limbs, it was almost inevitable that she became known as the Belarusian Swan.

But that was too easy. As if in reply to ballet-inspired comparisons, Svetlana performed for years to floor music that was rock 'n' roll or world beat, not classical. And she sometimes betrayed a lack of self-awareness that revealed just how instinctual her grace really was. Her short brown ponytail, clipped and sprayed into submission behind a roll of curled bangs, or escaping in wispy rebellion in spite of her efforts, seemed almost comically artless as a frame for those exotic eyes. More than that, though, she appeared not to know that her dance steps, although beautifully presented, came off as kooky and a little bizarre. She might walk with exaggerated flat-footedness, roll her shoulders, sway a hip—once, she even threw in a couple of froggy jumps with her feet flexed and knees splayed. Every routine contained at least one undulation (perhaps calculated to show off the preternatural flexibility of her spine), often imbued with thick hints of defiant eroticism. There was something baffling in the content of her gestures, and I think now that this is where I discerned the disjointedness of her personality, which I suspect is what gave rise to her artistry, and why she could not even see it.

As a teenager watching her on television, when I was a

gymnast too, and only two years her junior, I grew to revere her beyond all the more obvious foci of my adoration—that is to say, the Americans. The appeal of Mary Lou Retton and her ilk, like Phoebe Mills and Kim Zmeskal, hinged on their winning. The thing about Svetlana was that she was memorable whether she won or not. And she often didn't. There were years when she struggled, seemed too old or too defeated by bigger demons to bend gravity to her will. Over time she became like a signal coming through the noise.

Adolescence is the age of perfection in only a few realms, and gymnastics is one of them. I was twelve when I became a gymnast—a late start in that sport and the thing that, despite the talent I exhibited, effectively blocked me from ever becoming more than a varsity staple. I progressed from rolls to round-offs and flips and twists, landed spots on competitive club teams, and helped my high school win second in state. But I wouldn't go on to compete in college gymnastics. I didn't think I was good enough, and I probably wasn't. Yet what success I had was enough, because I wasn't really in it to win. I was in it for something much more necessary.

As spectators of sports, we project ourselves into our champions in acts of self-invention. We observe the best closely, and our favorites are often the ones in whom we find echoes of ourselves. When we see our champions win, we tell ourselves this means we can win too, despite our flaws, our failings, our inadequacies. Gymnastics was a world of absolute order and I wanted to believe I could fit into that order. But I never quite did. In Svetlana I saw a girl who aligned with my idea of what I wanted to be—pretty, serene, perfect—and simultaneously upended it. The essential mystery of her, that self-contradictory presentation, was rare in gymnastics, a sport that attracts more conventional personalities. Through Svetlana I sensed that there were others, other gymnasts, who felt chaos thrashing just beyond the edges of their tidy routines. Who even sometimes let it in.

I know now that Svetlana's own gymnastics story began at the age of six, when her parents first enrolled her in a class. A few years later she left her hometown of Minsk to live at a Soviet training center near Moscow, far from her family. By the time the renowned Soviet coach Lyubov Miromanova was preparing the fifteen-year-old for her first Olympics, Svetlana had lived with her for nearly half her life, subsumed into Miromanova's family as one of their own. By all accounts, Miromanova was a "surrogate mother" and "like a second mother" to the young gymnast. She led Svetlana to her first great victories—two gold medals at the '88 Games. Then, three days after returning home, Miromanova was found dangling from her apartment balcony. She had apparently hanged herself.

If any explanation for the suicide was uncovered, it never reached the American media. The cause remained a mystery to most, possibly even to Svetlana, who rarely spoke about it publicly. The following year, however, at the '89 World Championships, her floor routine reached its peak choreographic originality. Her dance moves included pausing dramatically for a beat or two to bang the air with her fists, as well as shaking her hands as if flicking water off them. At one point she even played an exaggerated air guitar—a move that is now legendary in gymnastics circles. An announcer noted that some judges objected that the routine was "too avant-garde." Another described her performance as "abstract and even disarming," musing aloud that it "seemed to reflect her inner turmoil" over Miromanova's death. I can't help but wonder what it must have taken for her to wear such confusion and pain on her body in world competition. But then, that might have been what made it possible for her to compete at all.

In interviews, Svetlana seemed a model Soviet, unfailingly team-minded and self-deprecating. But this was to some degree a fiction she wasn't always able to maintain. She was ferociously competitive and, by her own later admission, not above intimidating or bullying other gymnasts. I suspect, too, that loss and grief brought out the worst in her. In 1991 she made headlines for "snubbing" American gymnast Kim Zmeskal after losing to her at that year's World Championships, claiming that Zmeskal had failed to shake her hand the night before. The longtime coach of the American team, Bela Karolyi, was incensed and later recalled having found Svetlana "arrogant and nasty." But a year later, when a journalist asked about the incident as the 1992 Olympics approached, Svetlana seemed shaken by the memory and furtively wiped away a tear.

My losses, too, had made me eccentric—socially clumsy and prone to random, intense obsessions. I buried myself beneath a facade of conformity, and I suppose I paid for that. In high school, mental blocks rolled in. On balance beam, attempting the back tuck dismount, I froze. And froze, and froze. The move was easy for me in a physical sense. But with that hard wooden beam behind me, I never got past some wall of fear. Only in my imagination could I follow Svetlana's lead.

By the time Svetlana reached Barcelona, nineteen years old and leading the amalgam of former Soviets known as the Unified Team, announcers were describing her as a sort of team mother. I was by then one of the oldest gymnasts on my team, adored by the little girls and adoring them in return. When I practiced my jazzy floor routine, they would line up at the edge of the mat and dance my Charleston steps along with me. But I was also envious of how much better than me they already were, or clearly would become. During the preliminary rounds of the Barcelona competition, I was riveted by a shot of Svetlana comforting the tiny, fifteen-year-old Tatiana Gutsu—a star already and a superior gymnast in many ways—on the sidelines after a shocking fall from the balance beam. The horrified Gutsu, who completed moves so difficult that even today the skill level of her routines is rarely matched, was crying unabashedly. Svetlana wrapped her slender arms around the Ukrainian girl's neck and pulled her close. Her face, visible to the camera over the top of Gutsu's head, wore a look of stoically sympathetic calm. *Yes,* her eyes seemed to say, *I know.*

The best gymnasts walk a line between drama and control, the winners typically resolving the conflict through sheer physical power. Svetlana had this option only in her first few years in world competition. A gymnast's peak age is around fifteen, which Svetlana reached in 1988—the year of her first Olympics. By the early nineties, she was beginning to slip from her power-matches-prettiness niche, and few believed she could continue to hold her ground as a champion. The difficulty of her routines wasn't keeping up with the runaway progress of the sport. Even as she improved, the standards of the sport were rising much faster. Yet somehow, as this happened, she was becoming more compelling to watch.

Poring over videos of Svetlana's floor routines across three Olympics, from 1988 to 1996, I realize no one would guess that so many years lay between them. Her body remained the same elongated Y—shoulders twice as wide as her hips, her waist narrow and limber, all muscle and bone. Nearly her entire career as a global contender occurred while she was supposed to be on the decline. Her weaknesses, however, did begin to show. In the '92 European Championships, with her second Olympics on the horizon, she fell during the floor exercise on her final tumbling pass, a tucked double back. It was the most difficult floor routine of her career, but at the end she didn't get quite enough height. She landed short and lurched forward onto her knees, into an automatic half-point deduction. Many doubted that she could keep up with her teammates at the coming Olympics. She would have to rely on her dramatic lines to compensate for what were now, relatively speaking, unspectacular skills. Maybe the surprise was that the lines became the spectacle.

Following the progress of those Olympics on subscription Triplecast at a teammate's house, I passed a weekend anticipating Svetlana's routines with almost embarrassed intensity. As she stood ready to begin her floor exercise for the team final, it felt right that her uniform was black and white, its colors split diagonally across the front in a pattern suggesting lightning, or feathers. She sat down into an opening pose in which her back arched so that she was perched on the top of her head with her arms raised straight up—quintessentially dramatic and strange. Spanish guitar began to play. Then everything broke open. It was in the steps, the turns, that spine. It was in the way she could lace her movements with an edge so sharp that she seemed less like an athlete than an electrical storm. When she nailed her tucked double back, you felt it in your sternum. With that routine she led the Unified Team to victory.

But although Svetlana took home a team gold, she didn't medal in any of the individual event competitions or in the ultimate prize of the individual all-around. No one was surprised that after those Games, verging on twenty years old, she retired. Most gymnasts have one Olympics in them, maybe two. She moved to the United States and joined the professional exhibition circuit, touring as a performance gymnast, working the crowds at the gymnastics equivalent of the Ice Capades. I hated to watch her in those expos. To my eye, they parodied precisely what they were meant to valorize. She strutted onto the floor in a leather motorcycle jacket and a black baseball cap, as if to recall Marlon Brando in *The Wild One,* and all of it felt silly and reductive on a woman whose rebel music had been much more than a pop-cultural meme. She seemed not to see her own authenticity, not to grasp the scope of her reach.

Three years later I was in college, smoking weed and studying biology and listening to a lot of grunge. Having at last escaped the orbit of my mother's illness, I moved on to jogging and yoga and rarely talked about gymnastics anymore. The nearest I drew to that previous life happened only occasionally, late at night while walking home drunk from friends' parties, when just for kicks I would run suddenly to throw a tumbling pass on a nearby lawn. My friends, protective, tried to hold me back. There was no need. Those handsprings were embedded so deep in my cells that drunkenness couldn't touch them.

It wasn't until the Summer Games drew near again that I learned Svetlana was back. She had been training with the American team under Karolyi's tutelage and sprung back into world competition in 1995, competing for Belarus. After a tepid start, she did so well at the 1996 European Championships that she took home a silver all-around medal, qualifying her to compete in one last Olympics. She was twenty-three.

To return to that level of competition in that sport, at that age, after that long. It was the kind of amazing that maybe only a fellow gymnast could grasp—someone who had grown up as a gymnast and then already grown old as a gymnast. It was the kind of amazing that made your eyes flood. Svetlana would be one of the only female gymnasts ever to compete in three Olympics. In that land of perpetual girlhood, I had watched her leave girlhood behind. So I watched her again, out of love and loyalty and also, maybe, to learn something about womanhood now that our girlhood was gone.

In 1996, with the Unified Team disbanded, Svetlana seemed an avatar of a bygone era. One announcer said there had been talk that she couldn't have earned a spot on the Unified Team if such a powerful aggregate still existed. By then, younger gymnasts were flaunting skills that required physical strength of a kind that women's gymnastics had never seen before. Svetlana's later contemporaries, like Kerri Strug, blew judges away (and unnerved the sport's fairly conservative fan base) with the muscular builds that made possible their huge tumbling passes. Svetlana never put on that kind of muscle, and what's more, her prime time for skill acquisition was far behind her. She was already an adult. Making a quantum leap forward with the sport was simply not possible.

So she faced off against gymnasts who were nearly a decade younger than her, whom she towered above and, tipping the scales at about a hundred and ten, outweighed by some thirty pounds. The minuscule Dominique Moceanu, America's fourteen-year-old, four-foot-five-inch wunderkind, looked like a small child beside her. The benefits of smallness were clearer than ever, especially on beam, where Moceanu stuck a sequence of one back-handspring followed by *three* laid-out backflips. Such a string of tumbling moves would be impossible for a taller gymnast to fit within the length of the beam.

As it was, Svetlana nearly tipped off the end whenever she performed her usual sequence, which was identical to Moceanu's, minus one layout.

The effortlessness of her early tumbling was gone by then. Her skills were exceptional, but they often suggested how hard she was working. She responded by relying heavily on her twists and choosing choreography that highlighted both her originality and her maturity. The result was that, maybe more than ever, her perfection looked better than anyone else's perfection. She opened her floor exercise routine with the same full-in-back-out that she had performed in 1988 and closed with a two-and-a-half-twisting layout leading directly into a (perfect) punch front. Positioned confidently and moving smoothly, she made it look almost as if it were happening in slow motion. Up there in the air, as if at rest.

It was in her lines, those unbelievable joints, her timing. On bars the lines seemed to take over, with her individual skills almost reduced to links between moments of poetic pause. In moves that other gymnasts tended to pike, she almost suggested an arch. Watching the clip from the all-around competition, I get chills. In her giant swings, circling the high bar with her body fully extended, her shoulders roll back so far that the hinge at each joint disappears. And when, in a handstand at the top of the high bar, she spins around in a 360-degree pirouette (two in one routine), she is nearly airborne. Her double-layout dismount is like two breaths of wind.

The crowds were more in love than ever. People were calling her the Goddess of Gymnastics—a play on the Russian root of her last name, *boginya,* meaning "goddess." That week Svetlana got at least one standing ovation, and at times you could hear her name being chanted in the stands. But she won no medals. She lacked the necessary difficulty and made too

whether I was who I said I was. And whether I was trying to hurt her children. And Ann and I would talk about it and I'd say, "God, can you imagine how frightening that is?" And there's no doubt in my mind that she did believe it. I mean she just flat-ass believed it.

Did I say to myself, *Oh, she's becoming schizophrenic?* No. I didn't have a thought of anything like that. I just thought, *This is irrational, doesn't make any sense, and we're not going there.* I didn't know what it was.

I thought, *Well, you know, maybe it'll go away.* And it didn't.

. . .

I didn't know that there were medications. I didn't know there was a body of knowledge about it. I didn't know people could be treated and recover. And I didn't know that there was a variety of mental illnesses, each with its own characteristic pattern.

There was practically no understanding. People were referred to as being *crazy*. And that was a very bad thing. People who were crazy got locked up. It was almost a moral—there was kind of a stern feeling. If people were crazy, you didn't want them around. They should be taken care of discreetly somewhere else.

That was the basic default position: You just didn't notice it. It was a shameful condition. It was something that, like having a relative in the state penitentiary or—there was no understanding that it was an illness, that it was a treatable illness. And there wasn't a lot of sympathy either.

Those were the days when things like this happened because a mother's love was withdrawn or whatever. Nobody saw it as a chemical imbalance or anything like that.

More time passed, and it became clear that your mother was ill. And I didn't understand, I didn't understand the illness. I didn't understand how ill she was.

Now, is this supposed to come from one side of the brain?

And of course, your grandparents were pretty much in denial. Your grandfather was always trying to put a different explanation on it, which I understood more when Tom got sick because that's what I was doing, in retrospect. Trying to explain this behavior by every damn thing. *He's like me, I can remember going through that,* yada yada yada. You just don't want to believe it.

. . .

You know, my maternal uncle was psychotic—Perry, right. So there was mental illness in our family, but we avoided the subject. I think Mother faced it more than any of us. But she felt that burden of shame that people did in her generation, and she didn't talk about it. Didn't talk about Perry much.

I was in therapy. So a lot of times the therapist would say, "You know, your sister is mentally ill." And I would say, "No, no, that's the way she is." And they'd say, "No, this is different." So that gave me the confidence to say it to other people in the family.

I didn't know anything about anybody's mentalities, and I don't think Bob did either. He always thought she was sick, though, after she became delusional. I would be trying to convince her: "Mari, that couldn't possibly be true." And he would say to me, "Don't. She won't hear you." And she didn't. That was the hardest thing for me. To realize that anyone as bright as Mari could believe things that were absolutely unbelievable.

I think anybody who was around her found themselves feeling like *Okay, this is somebody who's mentally ill.* But what are you going to do about it? Because *she* doesn't want to do anything about it. So do you call up and have some kind of intervention where people come up with handcuffs and cart her off? I don't even think you can do that.

I think honestly I was in high school before I ever told myself that Mom has a mental illness. I don't think I ever thought of her like that. I don't think I was able to think of it like that.

I didn't really know what the terms meant, but I do remember once, I'd say something about Julie and she'd say, "Oh, well, you know, that's the other Julie. Not the real Julie." And I thought, *Whoa! That seems a little schizophrenic.* And she decided Chris was related to Queen Elizabeth. But I never cared. I just thought somebody should see her, and try to figure out what it is, and see if there are any medications that can help. You know, experiment. I just wanted somebody to experiment.

.   .   .

I've never really confided in anybody what it's like to have a schizophrenic mom. I mean, I'll talk to people about it. But there's just too many pieces. To me that's—that's in the therapy realm.

The first person I ever told was Lindsey. I remember being in the car, driving back from I think the mall, shopping. And I just got overwhelmed. Overwhelmed with kind of a grief. I remember putting my head down like this. I didn't realize I was doing that and then Lindsey was like, "Adrienne, are you okay?" And I was like, "Yeah, I'm fine." We went into Kim's house and I went up to Kim's room and I started crying. Crying and crying. Lindsey came up and was like, "What's wrong?" And I was like, "My mom is sick. My mom has an illness. My mom is mentally ill." It was the first time I ever said that out loud, to anybody. I was fifteen, I guess.

.   .   .

I'd seen a lot of similarities between me and Mari. I used to always say, "The difference between me and Mari is, there's this edge—of reality—and it's scary to me." I really, really felt I understood how she could see the edge. But I also had no interest. My instinct was to go the other way. If I got a sense I was getting close, I was like, *back*. She doesn't have that.

.

I've never really thought about how she receives it all. Whether she just comes up with this stuff, or actually does hear a voice that explains it.

I mean, you could see how they'd been constructed. At one point she told me that there were flying pigs at the ranch. And I happened to be in, I think it was Denver, and there were these big bus ads showing flying pigs, and I thought, *Maybe she picks up that kind of image and carries it around until she can fit it into a delusion.*

I think she understands that there are a lot of people in the world who don't believe these things are true, and she has to be pretty careful about those people. Because they're the ones who think that there's something wrong with *her*. And I think she puts me in that group.

Mostly I just resisted. I just felt like the situation was oppressive. Just always, knowing it wasn't her fault was a hard thing for me. Because knowing that, I felt a sense of obligation that I should be okay with it. And I wasn't.

It was a different kind of tension. It was just being in the flow of her illness, and really going with the flow of her illness. Constantly metering how present or non-present she was.

I think it's very hard for her to maintain normal for long. We go out to lunch, she gets so excited, you know, she gets dressed up. And then after fifteen or twenty minutes I have a feeling like, she's getting tense. It's getting hard to talk in a normal fashion and make normal conversation. I just feel badly. I say to myself, *Probably the best thing to do is just see her one-on-one. Keep it simple.*

I met a guy—he has a son in his fifties who's schizophrenic. We had a brief get-together and he said, you know, "We try to get them into our world and they try to get us into theirs." And this is what Tom did. And this is what your mother was doing.

.   .   .

I think both Mother and Dad really searched for why. And of course, it's an illness. You know, you don't feel that way about diabetes. But I think they will always, and maybe all parents will always try to figure out, *What was it?*

But you know, there's mental illness on Dad's side too. My aunt Helen had a serious breakdown as an adult. She had to be hospitalized. It was bad enough to affect who she was for the rest of her life. So I have always felt that Mother shouldn't feel like it's all on her side. And also I feel like this is good for you to know, because of genes.

I wish I could tell you more, but I really can't. As to what her brain was like, I haven't the faintest idea.

.   .   .

There are times it's irritating. She got on one about Jeff when we were getting married. Like, come on, I got a lot going on. I don't need you telling me that Jeff's going to jail in a month. That his ex-wife and he weren't divorced, and she had committed a crime, and he had said he would go to jail for her. Which is sweet. She likes Jeff. But I guess for all of us, it's a little less cute when it involves you personally.

I think she likes just very passing acquaintances. And people like her. And she is always so very neatly dressed, but very conservatively. In late years, I've thought people might take her for a little nun.

She's amazing. She's lived with us off and on. She's lived near me. And I have gotten frustrated. But it doesn't faze her. When she got upset with me, it *did* faze me—but when I've gotten upset with her, it's like just right over her head.

I do love her. But I find that her will is so powerful and inflexible and difficult to bend to—that's when I get into trouble. When I have to be with her for a period of time, I just start feeling like I've been run over, and I don't have any voice, and I have no opinions that count, and I start feeling really weird. It's the boundary thing. And she just mows you down. And that's not good.

She did tell me once I'm not who I think I am—but she likes me anyway. Which I thought was so touching. It really was.

. . .

I feel, gosh, she's missing so much.

But you know, it's weird. *We've* lost something. We've lost this person in a way, that was so dynamic and, in my opinion, brilliant. Somebody who was really, would stand up to anything she didn't agree with. And I think still does, but on a much—I don't know. I feel that there's so much about her I don't know.

You know, she doesn't want to change. This is who she is. And the Mari that I remember is just gone. There are parts of her, still. But I was just going to have to stop wanting her to be the way she was, because it wasn't ever going to happen. And now I feel like she's sort of this familiar stranger.

I think the way you have to look at it, the only way *I* can deal with it—you have to consider it a story. It's just what happened. It may not be the way you wanted it to be, but it is what happened. It's the way life is.

The Wildcatter

WHAT I KNOW OF MY MOTHER'S FATHER RESTS ON THE TAN-
gible. Objects such as the ones that filled his mansion at the
ranch in New Mexico that we called Circle Diamond, the family home, where he resided when he wasn't at his Los Angeles
offices or traveling for business. There were sleek leather sofas
and abstract paintings and Navajo blankets that smelled like
nothing but themselves—a smell that hit me once in a Santa
Fe rug shop and made me feel that he was there in the room.
It has always been as if through his objects he spoke to me,
though I do clearly recall his voice, soft and patient before a
stroke pulled down his words and slowed them to a warped
drone. It is the things, the touchable, graspable things, that
most seem to be from him, of him.

There is no reason why it should be this way. His life was
well recorded, more so than most. Journalists reported on him,
quoted him, in midcentury magazines and even a biography
he hired a reporter to write. The book is excellent or awful
depending on what you want from it. It contains many dates,
many numbers. But I am bad with dates, forgetful: He was
born in 1917 or 1918 or 1920. He died at the age of ninety

and I was there. I helped swab the dry lips once the unconscious body would no longer will the tongue to wet them, watched him exit the world. I remember the precise shape of his open mouth and how it stayed that way despite my uncle's efforts to close it once he was gone.

My overwhelming sense of him was whiteness. White hair, white Stetson, a preference for white foods like potatoes, vanilla ice cream. The unimpeachable whiteness of his Swedish lineage, so that nothing stood in the way of his rise. What particular Chicago neighborhood he came from, I can't say. But I know my family's immigrant stories, the rough shape of them just like so many other immigrant stories. The father gone to work as a bellboy at fourteen, working his way into banking. A gifted son, on scholarship at an elite school. Talent and charm. And then fortune came as fortune so often does in America, fast and beautiful.

Wildcatter is the word I most closely associate with him. *Wildcat,* used as a verb, then a descriptor. To go wildcatting. To be a wildcatter. One who wildcats. It brings to mind a creature, rangy and lean, point-eared, suggesting stealth, feline grace. In many ways this is the wrong image. Wildcatting is prospecting for crude oil—analyzing the geology of an area and then drilling test wells where the rock is the right age and formation to signal the possible presence of a reserve. Being a wildcatter required intelligence, perseverance, nerve. But there was also the glamour of the oil business in the age of the automobile, and the word captured that glamour.

His full climb took decades, started with one refinery. Unglamorous, situated in a small town in the western desert— a place that at first felt barren and lonely to my grandmother. But with some fine-tuning and a few innovations it kept him flush enough to buy more refineries, then a plane. He hopped around the West, well to well, dig to dig—years and years when wildcatting was more like a bad habit than a job, years of failures when all the money came from the faithful refineries. He once said that he must have dug two hundred dusters before he hit his first gusher.

This is where the story begins to sweep me away, invariably, and I lose track of what I might have intended to critique. I am along for the ride, repeating the myth as it has always been repeated. Because it still stands in for history, and because it is thrilling and potent and it makes me feel—here it is, the bare truth of it—special.

I know the names of the biggest oil fields, the biggest events. Empire Abo, that first gusher. Then the major purchases, the business deals. Atlantic Refining Co., in Philadelphia. Richfield Oil, in Los Angeles. The merger he orchestrated, creating the Atlantic Richfield Company, ARCO—I've hunted down the year: 1966. The logo I have known forever—a square that is tilted to resemble a gemstone, facets cut through with curved lines that suggest freeways, forward momentum. I first saw it decorating the highball glasses in the Big House at the ranch, or painted on the sides of private jets I was sometimes ushered into. And the name—ARCO, all-caps, Helvetica font—emblematic of an era, an ideal, a belief that the progress of modernity was arriving, exactly then, at its ultimate destination.

The twin pillars of the old ARCO Towers and Plaza rise in parallel from the northwest side of Flower Street in Los Angeles, close enough to the 110 freeway that they are among the most visible skyscrapers in the city, easily seen by anyone skirting downtown. Their design is what I have always called "seventies architecture," though I only saw them for the first time as an adult, never having visited my grandparents at their beachside apartment. The towers are, officially, Corporate International style—solid shapes of dark glass and deep green marble, squares within rectangles, a grid of straight edges, tall plain boxes, unattractive at a distance. Even up close, the polished stone offers little purchase. The buildings are not welcoming—the scale is unforgiving, their simplicity severe. But if you walk through the plaza between them and go around the wide porticoes to the back, you find that there the buildings are sunken beneath street level so that it is quiet, and the dark stone benches in the garden echo back the street sounds so that they come like the striking of distant chords. Here the broad rectangles of the benches and columns form peaceful geometries, separating trees and gardens of long grasses and occasional bursts of flowers blooming orange-red, the color of the sculpture between the buildings, at the center of the plaza.

The sculpture rests on short posts that descend, nearly invisibly, into a round, shallow pool, so that it seems to hover on the water. It is a bright and smooth-surfaced structure, consisting of two spiral-staircase-shaped segments that wind up from opposite sides of the pool toward one another until they meet at the top, long edge to long edge. Two sets of eighteen steps that slowly twist into an architectural embrace. The thing is beautiful, intriguing, exciting. The shape you see changes utterly as you walk around the plaza. Here it is broad, with the space between the two shapes forming an archway that I would surely walk through if it weren't for the water. From other angles it is a tight, compact, energetic helix that bulges in different places depending on your position. I love it absolutely.

The sculpture was created by my grandfather's friend, a Bauhaus designer who first titled it *Stairway to Nowhere*. This is the title I have always remembered, though the name was quickly changed to *Double Ascension*. I have read that "corporate executives rejected" the first title because it "did not reflect company goals." This doesn't sound like something my grandfather would say. In fact, he liked *Stairway to Nowhere*, its irreverence. He believed in art that challenged you, that asked you to consider alternate perspectives. Perhaps it was others who objected, and he acquiesced.

Walking across that plaza for the first time a few years ago, having made a point of visiting it while in Los Angeles for a conference, I commented to my friend Curran that the place made me remember how it felt to be part of my grandparents' world, and what it is that money buys the very wealthy: the luxury of comfort anytime, anywhere. It's in the way the rest of the world moves around you so that you may stay comfortable even while everyone else does not. You have your private plane, your fleet of servants, everyone taking care of everything for you, everything happening when you want it to happen. There is a peace and calm in the world of the very rich that does not exist anywhere else. I first tasted it during vacation visits to my grandparents—an open, soothing sensation that hung in the air around them—and I felt it for a moment in that plaza too. Just an echo, just enough to call them to mind. I noticed also that the ceilings of the porticoes at the bases of both towers were covered in a seemingly random pattern of small beige mosaic tiles. And these were the same tiles that lined the swimming pool at the ranch, except that those were blue. And this detail made me feel suddenly that my grandfather was right there—that this really *was* his piece of displaced sky, and he really did pass his days in an office on the fifty-first floor of the north tower, taking in a view that must reach many miles out to sea.

But that is the view from inside, and that is not where I am anymore. I have lived too many years apart from that buffered world. What I want to speak of now is what you see when you have been both inside and outside. What I want to say is that I went to Los Angeles and walked around the ARCO Towers and found them grand and terrible, and I have since felt unable to untwine the one sensation from the other.

By the time I was old enough to know what questions to ask, my grandfather's speech was labored and slow. A blood clot let loose during bypass surgery had lodged in his brain, causing a stroke that weakened and limited him for the last fifteen years of his life. His mind remained sharp right up to the end, however, and he was patient, had always been patient. I listened closely as he worked his way carefully through his sentences, knowing it was worth the wait. His memory was uncanny, his stories enchanting. But in hindsight I see that there was also a lot of name-dropping, a lot of shiny packaging. I loved best the anecdote about Truman Capote: Over lunch one day, Capote had watched a fly buzz about for half an hour and then said he could trace its exact path by memory. Perhaps I selected this story to love best because it was the least implicating. Other men my grandfather had been friendly with came up looking less rosy in the backlight of history: Nixon, the Shah of Iran. Men in business and politics, men whose crimes still haunt us.

In my life, the money was always distant. My father insisted it be this way, that we live off only what he could earn. So we did, and wealth was a phantasm I could fly into as into a storm each summer when we visited the ranch, where I was a farmhouse landing in Oz, playing awhile in my grandparents' Technicolor world before returning to waking life. They regularly came to me too—to Anchorage, where they rented a suite on the top floor of the Hotel Captain Cook and held dinner parties at its long table, eating food ordered through room service and served by waiters from carts draped in white cloth. It was not until high school that I grasped the salient relationship between the place and the man—that Alaska meant something to my grandfather because there was oil there. That he meant something to Alaska because he had found the oil and delivered it to the world. And that this was, indirectly, how Alaska came to be my home.

Prudhoe Bay was his greatest find, the *largest oil field ever discovered in North America*. These words I memorized decades ago. They are part of the myth. They are its punch line, really, the end point of his story about the North Slope and its deep secrets. The story goes that other companies—BP and Sinclair—were also prospecting there, and that they, too, were convinced that its geology indicated there must be something down there to find. Logistics were a nightmare—the Arctic Ocean froze solid every winter, and there were no roads in the entire northern half of the state. Obstacles were overcome and wells were drilled. Came up dry. Again, again. One by one the other companies pulled out. It was too expensive, too risky. But ARCO stayed on until there was no one else left. It was time to give up. My grandfather said, "Dig one more." And that was the drill that found the reserve at Prudhoe Bay.

I would like to know if this story is accurate. I do not know who to ask. Everyone I know to ask tells this same story. It is the story as he told it. It is the story as the book tells it. Surely, then, the facts are correct. It is just that there is something else about the story that doesn't sit right, that has never sat right with me. It is that this is the story of a man congratulating himself. And so there is no way to trust it.

Later I came to prefer my grandmother's versions of such

and long, straight noses—each ten feet tall and weighing one and a half tons. They were torn from the structure one by one in a process that, by necessity, broke them in half. The figures were severed at the hip joints, leaving only the head and torso and the upper part of the wings. Afterward, the wrecking company sold them off for the cost of removing them—one hundred dollars each. The current whereabouts of most of the figures are unknown. One ended up in the downtown loft of a graphic designer who bought it from an elderly client, a man who had long ago purchased it from the wrecking company. Moving it required hiring a crane and a forklift. It was so heavy that he had to have a special base constructed for it.

I was surprised to learn that my grandfather had actually torn such a building down, had pushed ahead with it. This wasn't the story I knew. I thought of the Big House at Circle Diamond, its collections of artifacts of the West and its people, rescued from decay. For a long time, I couldn't square it. The Richfield Building has since been called a masterpiece, a lost treasure. Architects don't necessarily agree. Some thought it gaudy, with that garish neon lettering, and it certainly lacked nuance. But it was beautiful in many ways and striking from a distance. It has long since been named one of the "most missed" demolished buildings in Los Angeles, and its loss is widely regarded as a travesty—made worse by the insult of replacing it with two blockish glass rectangles that, for the most part, do little to recommend themselves.

My grandfather's vision, at least, was grand. The new complex was modeled after Rockefeller Center, with an underground shopping mall that linked the towers and was accessible by escalators from the street. It was meant to be active, a hub, drawing people in from all around. Still, destroying the Richfield Building didn't sound to me like something he would do—even though it was done, according to another executive, "with tears in our eyes." When I told people I didn't get it, they gave me the same replies: *It was that era. It was the thinking of the time.* But, I kept thinking, he wasn't like other oilmen. He gave to the arts and to universities, funded research on alternative energy, championed land conservation. He was an intellectual.

The ARCO Towers—their size and significance, at least—were unknown to me until well into my adulthood. My family is large and diffuse, and my mother, struggling with mental illness, cut herself off from her parents for decades. She took us to see them on occasion, but mostly we stayed in their houses when they were not there. She never told me any stories about them, never explained much about who they were or what it meant. What I knew came mostly from my father, in scattered pieces, incomplete. And it came from what I absorbed, uncritically, of the objects in the houses we visited—the Big House at the ranch, the Red House in Aspen, the condo in Santa Fe. The dozens of paintings and drawings my grandfather commissioned—landscapes of his ranches and portraits of the pretty faces of daughters, sons, their wives. And other works he bought at auction—all manner of abstracts, oils, and sketches from Renaissance workshops.

One college summer break, during a few weeks with Curran in Ventura County, we spent a day at the Los Angeles County Museum of Art. Entering the building that housed its modern and contemporary collection, I looked up and saw my grandfather's name on its exterior wall. The building, which was added on to the original museum in 1986, was named after him. I knew nothing of this, so Curran pulled me to the admissions desk to ask the clerk for details, to confirm that indeed this was my grandfather. The clerk gushed for a few minutes and then gave me a free ticket. She was thrilled. I was thrilled.

But as time passed, the memory of that experience and others disoriented me. The way money inspired extreme responses—enthusiasm or animosity, not much in between. I was afraid to be the object of animosity, but neither did I understand the enthusiasm. I could see that people liked to be near money, or near someone who, like me, was near money— that there was vicarious pleasure in that. But I saw, too, that while money elevated me in some eyes, it brought out a cold burn in others. This was the part I wanted to disavow. The money was not mine—it belonged to my grandparents. And yet it had made me subtly different from everyone I knew, in ways I could only barely see. It did not occur to me that some-day there might be millions for me. Not then and not for sev-eral years after, not until other questions led me to finally put together that I would eventually have been given a share that was, by middle-class standards, enormous. But this is just as well, because by the time that day came, the fortune was gone.

In retrospect I can see that money's insidious power lies precisely in the objects that it buys. It lies in the capacity of the tangible to validate the intangible. My grandparents' money placed rewards all around us, all day long—physical, observable rewards. And the mind's subterranean logic so eas-ily takes this to mean that we are deserving. Not, perhaps, more deserving than all others. But deserving nonetheless. This is how money makes the wealthy believe they are right in their choices, their opinions, their attitudes. It validates those choices simply by providing objects that reflect all this back at them, leading them to believe that there is an inherent and undeniable rightness about them. It happens unconsciously. There is no getting around it.

It was not until I discovered that my own hard work would often come without rewards that I could see this—not until I discovered firsthand that money is not an inevitable result of being good, doing good, working hard. That the economics of the twenty-first century do not reliably deliver wealth, or even a decent living, for many skills and talents. And although I was born into that feeling of rightness, over the years I have felt it erode, bit by bit. And now I fight to hang on to it. Because it looks like success and it feels like confidence. I fight by keeping around me the objects of my memories. Some paintings my grandparents left behind. An oil portrait of my mother. And a favorite large abstract that I used to stare at in the Santa Fe condo, the one that now resides in my stairwell on the only wall in the house that is large enough to hold it.

Walking north from the ARCO Towers on that day with Curran a few years ago, past a handful of other corporate skyscrapers from that era, I could see that it was fairly standard to place a large sculpture in an open space before the building. Curran commented, as we passed two different ones, that they were stunningly, comically phallic. Tall, tilted, narrow. The second, which was also cylindrical, seemed so obvious that I couldn't understand how it could have ever been *not* obvious. It featured several loops of metal swirling at its base in a way that strikingly suggested pubic hair. We laughed out loud, but as we walked on, my laughter gave way to a jagged relief that these were not my grandfather's buildings, that his plaza's sculpture was nothing like these. And I wondered about how such obvious things can so easily go unseen. How it ties in to something about power, and men, and money, and complicity. Something irreducible about the flow of energy in the world, about who directs the flow and why.

I have a way of talking about the things my grandfather did: He built the Trans-Alaska Pipeline. He built the Towers. He *built* them. But what I mean is that he orchestrated the building of them, or financed the building of them, or decided that they would be built. The work was done by someone else's hands. And yet, with *built*, I claim this work as his own. I conflate idea and action, order and obedience, boss and employee. It is a kind of synecdoche, in which the man at the top stands in for all who hold him up. They are *of* him—aspects, expressions, manifestations of his will. I have not intended to do this, have not realized I do this.

Now I am tangled, caught in a tangle. I know that I, too, am one of the subsumed. Along with my grandmother, five aunts and two uncles, their wives and husbands, my many cousins, his employees, and the staff who kept his households running—Mexican ranch hands, black servants. Maids, housekeepers, gardeners, cooks, and the nanny who cared especially for my mother, a woman we called "Lala." The small, dark woman my mother trusted, I suspect, above all others. Lula Webster. That was the woman's name. I want you to know her name.

I know that my grandfather fancied himself like an English lord, and grew broad, manicured lawns around the Big House to mimic those at a manor. There was a white gazebo near the creek and peacocks that wandered around the grounds, dropping iridescent feathers for us children to gather. I know that the family portrait he commissioned, which hung not long ago on loan in a museum, features all seven of his children but only two of their spouses—the sons' wives. It is a complex composition, with eleven people positioned among rocks and trees, and at the visual center, where the eye is drawn, are the two most attractive daughters. All his daughters' husbands are notably absent. They were not, apparently, part of his domain.

In my mind I scroll through the secret history of my grandfather: his parties, his affairs, my grandmother's humiliation—which almost ended their marriage. I have heard stories, half told, guardedly, or received thirdhand via cousins: my youngest aunt, college-aged, finding him skinny-dipping with her friends. Or how, in the late eighties, my grandmother nearly left him after he was sued for child support by another woman—for his eighth child, a daughter. From their personal accounts he would pay many thousands each year to support the girl. So I have a half aunt who is roughly the same age as I am—English, of all things, from London, where my grandfather had an office for a while and a mistress about the age of his youngest girls. I think sometimes of this ghost aunt, would like to meet her, to know what she knew or remembered of him. But I won't try to find her. To do so I would have to ask questions that others would not want to answer.

I still sometimes tell the story of meeting Qaddafi. Still say to myself, *I've been ogled by Qaddafi.* Maybe I want to track the feelings—the quiet that falls over me, the stillness settling in. And the surges of anger that come sometimes too, toward my grandfather, even toward Will for his glib reaction to the revelation. I want to track the memories of my grandfather's way with women. His benign dismissals. His flirtations with secretaries. A cousin once glancing sidelong at me and saying, "He even flirts with his *granddaughters.*" The moments, back before the stroke, when he used to catch my eye across the room and wink as if there was a secret between us. The mischief, the attention—being singled out, noticed. That was why

all his daughters could say they felt close to him. And I want
to track all of this because it seems to mean something that is
maybe the key to this composition. It is in the way powerful
men can warp reality, bending it around them so that others
see only what they themselves see. It almost seems like a pas-
sive process: Reality simply bends *for* them, and they accept
this about it and so does everyone else.

Events would come to be marked, in family shorthand, as
occurring before or after my grandfather *lost all his money*.
As if the line of demarcation was clear, its implications known.
How it happened was unremarkable, really—as much an ordinary feature of capitalism as his dramatic success had been.
ARCO had gone public, had grown unwieldy, wasn't light
and flexible, as my grandfather liked things to be. Markets
shifted. Prices fluctuated. There were more mergers. The company diversified, lumbered along, lost stock value. He turned
sixty-five, retired as CEO. At sixty-eight, he stepped down
from the board. He wanted to return to what had made his
blood quicken, so he started a new company with his sons,
a smaller one, and got back into wildcatting. And that's it—
that's the story. He did what he had always done, leveraging
his assets heavily to pay for these endeavors. But the gamble
didn't pay off, at least not before the stroke suddenly ended
his career. There was no second Prudhoe Bay, or anything that
came close, only a natural gas field in Colombia that was just
big enough to cover his debts if he sold off everything else,
including his stake in ARCO. The fortune was gone. He had
lost it the same way he made it: looking for oil.

It seems that the pair of skyscrapers at Fifth and Flower
did, for a while, fulfill my grandfather's hopes for them. But

the future he envisioned did not last long. Urban decay and their own monolithic design conspired against it. ARCO sold the buildings to a real estate firm in 1986 and, in 1999, as a cost-cutting measure, moved out of the eleven floors it had occupied. By 2003, the place was nearly half empty, and its underground mall, which had many shuttered storefronts, was notably gloomy. In 2006, the complex ceased to be known under the name ARCO, its moniker changed to reflect that of a new corporate tenant. The new owners did promise to renovate and find ways to revive the complex, but ultimately their changes accomplished little to that end. Among other things, one of the owners considered adding some kind of light-show feature—an idea inspired by his childhood memories of the giant red neon letters on the old Richfield Building.

My family no longer owns any part of ARCO, which is now a fraction of its former size since being broken apart some years ago, the remainder bought up by BP Amoco. Around then the building at LACMA that housed modern and contemporary art was repurposed and renamed, my grandfather's appellation removed from its wall. The buildings and the company have moved on. I do not think the family expected this. Most of the ranch, too, had to be sold off after his stroke rendered him too fragile to earn back what he had lost. The family did keep, until very recently, two old adobe houses and a field that once were part of Circle Diamond, and when I went there I could still pick apples from the orchard, spot wild turkeys, and watch a few dozen head of cattle graze. But the Big House belonged to a Texas banker who was never there. I used to sometimes walk through the old property, peeking into the windows of the mansion, remembering where my grandfather kept the old convertible Cadillac and where the peacocks roosted in the evenings when darkness fell. The place had defined our family, and so for a long time it still felt like ours.

I eventually understood that what separated my grandfather's wild success from his subsequent failure was little more than luck—that the first time around, for a good four decades, he had been profoundly, phenomenally lucky. Not just in the specific sense of drilling in the right spot but in a general sense—lucky to be starting out in America in the middle of the twentieth century, lucky to be white and male, lucky to be interested in oil at the moment the world was most deeply in love with it, lucky to ride that wave as long as he did.

I know that at his peak, in the early 1980s, *Forbes* listed his net worth at $400 million. I know this because my father told me long ago. I have carried this number with me ever since, keeping it tucked in a fold in my mind, awaiting the day when I will make sense of it. Of what it meant to be a man who made $400 million, who lost $400 million. Of what it means that such sums can be won and then forfeited in a single lifetime. Of who I am, as one whose legacy is the memory of an enormous fortune, tangentially experienced and unexpectedly lost. To me this has become a parable, a fairy tale of ephemerality. I think occasionally that nothing could be more appropriate, nothing could be more American.

The Dragon at the Bottom of the Sea

THE BUS FROM SAN JOSE TAKES FOREVER, BUT I DON'T CARE.
I'm not thinking about much and my brother isn't talking
much. Stepping off at the stop in our first Costa Rican beach
town, Tom and I walk with our tall backpacks down the dusty
yellow road toward the center of Tamarindo. Passing under
a sign for a hotel named after the town, he says, "Hey look:
Tom-Marin-Do." He smiles, pleased with his observation.
I beam at him, at his odd cleverness and, more than that,
because it feels like for a moment he has come near to me.

It is 2002. I'm twenty-seven and still living as I have since
college—season by season. I plan to linger with Tom in Costa
Rica for several weeks before we work our way down to Panama for Christmas, to join our father and sisters in Bocas del
Toro. Because someone needs to spend some time with Tom
and I am the one who can. I'm single, with a seasonal job.
And he trusts me.

The road is lined with concrete buildings and restaurant
patios. It ends in a roundabout with a park bench in the middle, an entrance to the beach at our right, a side street to our
left, and an open-fronted, thatch-roofed bar directly in front

of us, where a good-looking young Rasta man lounges by the door.

Not far down the side street we find a cheap backpackers' motel, a crumbling one-story compound recommended in our Lonely Planet guide. We get a dark, airless room with two small mattresses on springs, a couple of low tables, and an electric fan. Old sheets cover the window, which looks out on the street and across the blazing day toward more dingy concrete buildings. "This is perfect," I tell him. All the other rooms are taken by young surfers and travelers, the kind who spend six months wandering through five countries. Our kind, I tell myself. I take comfort these days in the things I tell myself.

Tom is three years younger than me, a good-looking kid with a square jaw, a wide smile, and almond-shaped hazel eyes—a kind of hazel that shifts in concentric rings from blue to green to yellow to orange to brown. I sometimes say he has rainbow eyes.

Tom is delightful in a sharp-witted way, with a rangy intellect and a habit of passing the time talking about Picasso, Conrad, Bruce Lee. A couple of years ago he made twenty thousand dollars day-trading on the Internet, and I like to joke about how we'll spend his money when he's a millionaire. A lean, strong twenty-four-year-old, he climbs mountains too, and the rocks around Boulder, where he has lived since he left home to attend the University of Colorado. He has also done things like bike through Europe and scale the icy Alaskan crag known as the Moose's Tooth. This last one in particular is a point of pride for me.

I like to tell people these things, but I really don't care what he does as long as he's Tom. We have an easy, deep bond that has to do with the way he is more like me than either of our two sisters. By that I mean how he thinks—equally analytical and intuitive. A couple of years ago, watching us finishing one another's sentences while deciphering the instructions for a GPS device, a friend made the comment that we had the same brain.

But we don't. Unlike me, Tom seems fearless. I'm hyper-sensitive, easily overwhelmed. When I feel strong emotions, I go numb. And for the past few years, winter's darkness has been shutting me down. I have a lot of feelings about the brain, most of which I can't articulate. What I know about the brain is not information I recall in a way that lends itself to sharing. It is remembered in my body, and when it comes to the surface it does not come in words. It takes me back to our mother's house, where we took care of each other by escaping together into imagined worlds.

In truth, my life doesn't look so different from his, working and traveling intermittently as I do. I have a good gig going, spending the summer season in Alaska banding birds for Fish & Wildlife, passing my winters skiing in Montana and travel-ing in Asia or Latin America. But I don't like my life nearly as much as everyone thinks I ought to. I am plagued by loneliness or something like it. Moving each season keeps me solitary, alone with everything I have not yet learned how to say out loud.

Tom has always seemed immune to the sensitivities that afflict me, so I have a special kind of faith in him, in his smarts and his nerve. Except that Tom has not climbed any moun-tains in about a year. He has dropped out of college, too, and lost most of the money he made day-trading when the market turned. Since then he has not been doing much at all.

I have invited Tom to come down with me early, travel-ing one-on-one, so I can watch him closely and see what is happening—if *it* is happening. If it is happening, I'll know it when I see it, because it happened to our mother. It is obvious if you know what it looks like. That is the idea anyway. None of us have put much thought into this. Thinking is hard, because the thought of *it* wraps us in a kind of mental static.

Outside on the porch I sit for a few minutes on a wooden bench and watch the street life beside a dour Israeli surfer. He's had something stolen. Thieves all over this town. "Wild, wild West," he says.

I meet Tom down at the beach, where he is sitting with the Rasta and looking stoned. I'm distracted because the Rasta, a Jamaican–Costa Rican who introduces himself as Carlos, is hot. He has a surfer's ripped torso, black shoulder-length dreads, and a loose, unbuttoned shirt with flames coming up the sides. Sitting on the sand, I look out over low splashing waves and water that is bright with the lowering sun. The beach is straight and long, and full of young men in board shorts and tribal tattoos and women in bikinis and Lycra surf shirts. We sit with Carlos for a while and he flirts with me, charming and playful and direct, but I am hungry, so Tom and I go. Tom has bought some weed already.

The people on the beach are American, Italian, French, Argentine, Chilean, Canadian, Australian, Israeli, Spanish, Costa Rican. The people on the beach are the people at the parties. The DJs are Italian or French and the music is European dance trance mashed up with Manu Chao or Jamaican dancehall. The parties happen Tuesday, Wednesday, Thursday, Friday, Saturday night, in the little bars and the big bars and the other places at the edge of town with dance floors and swimming pools and I don't even know what they are when they're not hosting the parties.

beating the wall with the muscle of his shoulder as he goes, making it violently shake.

Melvin climbs up beside me, starts talking in English. "Jump in!" I tell him. I'm trying not to keep looking at him, but I keep looking at him.

"I could!" he says, his face fierce. Then he's quiet, and he doesn't.

Anyone can jump in and run around while the bull and his rider leap and turn and flail. When a rider gets thrown, the rodeo clowns and whoever else is in the pen swoop in to pull him by the shoulders away from the hooves and the horns. But it's not really the hooves and the horns that get me. It's the meat, the sides of meat, the muscle power, the force of such a thick animal hurtling through space.

The pounding of the meat of the bull against the logs seems to wake something up in my body. Some knowledge coming through the static, through the pervasive numbness that has enfolded me so thickly in recent months. And for a moment I'm aware of it, just barely—a trickle of electricity, pushing through the numbness, bringing me back into myself some-how, reminding me that these limbs and this mind are of the same being. I feel alive again—just briefly, until I climb back off the logs and the feeling is gone.

Tom and I buy a used surfboard and take turns on it. We've both surfed only a few times. Tom, stronger in the upper body, catches on much more quickly than I do. Except that he doesn't have much focus these days.

I start out okay, but I only seem to get worse. I keep get-ting pounded. I find myself up on the board with the wave hurling me forward, and I feel the rush and the white foam advancing over the water and for a moment I'm as elated as

I've ever been. But I can't hang on to it. I can't stay with it, really—closely, the way you have to. I can't feel the water beneath me, listen to it, let it tell me what to do. So I fall, hard, and it bangs me under and under. And when it does I just roll, flop, bounce, scrape, stand up again, and go back for more. At some point I tell myself that I'm doing something wrong, but I don't try to fix it.

I compensate by looking great. I am tan and lean and my long hair is streaked with blond, and I walk around in bikini tops and short shorts. Carlos at the Rasta bar keeps coming on to me, but for some reason I resist him. It has something to do with the fact that he sells weed to my brother, that my brother went and found him before I found him, so now they are attached in my mind.

There's no pot left. Tom's getting ready to go find Carlos to score some more. He has killed the whole stash, minus the few puffs I took when he offered.

Tom tells me he has recently become much more disciplined about his athletic training. When I ask what he means, he says he's planning to swim from Alaska to Japan. He has been preparing for this by thinking about swimming, extensively, by visualizing swimming across the Pacific for hours at a time.

Now when I go out to the beach I usually go alone. Tom surfs occasionally but goes out by himself. More often, he stays in our little room, smoking pot in the dark. I fetch him at dinnertime. When I switch on the lights, he sits up and looks at me with a Cheshire cat grin and starts telling me about what he's been doing all afternoon.

"I've been building matrices," he says. "I'm getting good at it. This one I did today! Wow. It was so cool." He shakes his head in disbelief. "It was so amazing." I ask him what the matrices are like.

"Well, this one today, it started out as just a cube. I always start with just a cube. And then I made it glow, like neon, green. And I expanded it into two cubes, and then I multiplied those, and then I gave the cubes more angles. And it turned blue. Then I, like, added another matrix to that one, started forming this pyramid, and then I started turning it around, and as it turned it changed colors, like the whole rainbow. It was amazing. So cool." He's smiling inwardly, chuckling to himself as he speaks, rolling his eyes in awe. He has spent the whole day in here, doing this.

"So you're imagining these matrices?" I ask. And he says "Yeah," but in a way that's not quite convincing. It makes all the difference: Either the matrices seem real but he knows they're not, or they seem real and he does not know, no longer knows, that they're not. I'm trying to discern whether Tom has crossed a line, into the mental territory to which he is pressing so near. What I'm trying *not* to do, on the other hand, is acknowledge what I've known for weeks—that I already have the answer. That I had seen and heard enough to know it even in Anchorage, before we headed down here, and have since just been telling myself that I can't be certain, I can't say for sure.

I am beginning to notice the crackheads. They linger at the roundabout and the bar where Carlos works. They are all *ticos* in their twenties and thirties, twitchy messes. I try not to stare, but I'm fascinated by them. One guy, everyone calls him Mono. Monkey. He's lanky, with cropped hair, and the form of his mouth sticks way out. When I sit on the café patio that faces out toward the water and read my ridiculously out-of-context novels—Edith Wharton, Henry James—he taps his temple, nodding approvingly. *"Inteligente,"* he says. *"Qué bueno."* I sink at the thought of my stalled life, and his stalled brain.

Lining the road near the roundabout are all kinds of blankets where people sell trinkets and other stuff. I peruse them with a girl I've befriended, who has a tattoo of a flowering tree that climbs all the way up her calf. There's one crackhead whose merchandise delights her. He sells paintings. He's got dozens of them, unstretched canvases that he keeps in a big roll and flips through for you. He can apparently get his hands on only three colors of paint, and those colors are green, yellow, and black. Everything is in green, yellow, and black. The scenes seem to be the kind he thinks tourists will go for. Lots of dolphins, leaping out of limpid water and catching the moonlight.

The paintings are amazing. They are ugly beyond ugly. They encounter new, distant continents of ugly. My friend wants one. We walk up and she asks how much.

"A hundred dollars," he says. She blinks.

"Oh," she says. "Well, thank you." We turn away and he leans forward.

"Five dollars!" he says. She turns back, considering, then decides that five dollars is too much, and we leave.

Melvin, the *tico* from the rodeo, doesn't notice me until he notices that I want him. I'm at one of the big bars with some people I've picked up somewhere. Tom is at the motel. I almost feel like I'm traveling solo now, like I didn't come to this town with anyone but myself, except that I often end up hanging out with people Tom befriends by offering them a toke. Every evening after dinner a streak of panic runs through me as I head out, wondering if I'll have companions or if I'll end up alone. During the day I prefer to be alone for hours at a time, to read and surf and lie in the sun. And I seem to be incapable of making plans, relying instead on just showing up and finding acquaintances in the places I'm likely to come across them. It's easy, because travelers befriend each other instantly.

I meet a lot of Americans who come for only a week. They stay at the nice hotels and think Tamarindo is great fun, and they make shocked observations about things like the brothel and the crackheads, or they laugh about things like the brothel and the crackheads, and I despise them. I try to find the people who are making their way down the continent or have been here three times before. This works well most of the time, but occasionally there is no familiar face anywhere and I find myself trolling the streets at nine at night. Then for a moment the static coheres, and I feel myself suddenly— thickly, insistently—desperate for somewhere to land. I cannot go back to the motel room and sit there with Tom. Not when it's dark out. If I sit in that room with him when it's dark out, then the darkness begins to eat me alive and the bare yellow light bulbs begin to glow sulfurous and mean, and my whole life appears cruel and sad.

I see Melvin across the bar and lock eyes with him a few times. Then as I'm leaving with a couple of other people, wondering whether to drink or smoke a little more, he appears from behind us and starts talking. He's asking us where we're going. It's late but not late. I know another place, he says. Then the other people go on home and I'm with him at this other place, a large, square bar I've never been to, where he buys me a beer and I stand and watch while he plays pool. I find myself wishing his name wasn't Melvin. How awkward,

I think, that I'll have to tell people I hooked up with a guy named Melvin. I'll have to apologize for it, say, *Yes, well, in Spanish the name doesn't sound as bad.*

Strangers don't see what I see happening to Tom. He doesn't talk to them about matrices and jaw detachments. He has bought one of those shirts with flames up the sides, and his brown hair is growing longish and reddish and thick. On the bench facing the dusty street, he offers new arrivals a toke, and then instantly they're his friends. He mostly befriends men, probably because that doesn't require as much talking.

"Your silent brother," the girl with the tattoo of the flowering tree calls him. I can tell she thinks he's cute, and when he ignores her, her appetite for pursuit surfaces. At lunch at a long wooden table on a café patio, she makes a game of trying to get him to speak to her. But he just doesn't. She laughs about it. I feel the need to offer an explanation.

"He's a genius," I say when Tom turns away, and half believe it myself when I hear it come out of my mouth. How amazing that would be if it were true. If that were the reason behind his behavior. In my mind, extraordinary intelligence somehow becomes the answer, the solution to this awful problem.

My friend is impressed. So are the two Canadians we're with, a blond hippie girl and a weird guy with a guitar and a bright yellow T-shirt. I love that they are impressed. They peer over at him, thrilled. I can see the wheels turning in their minds as they consider the implications of his genius. What might be going on inside that brain. Things they could never imagine.

At some point I begin to allow the word to reside in my head, and a thought that becomes too insistent: The thing about schizophrenia is that once it happens, it just keeps happening.

Every day, Tom is there in that motel room, getting stoned and hallucinating. He surfs less and less. Mostly he lounges in the motel courtyard and in the room. He does little more than watch the visions in his head. When he's not stoned, he talks about the visions. They've been happening for months. They happen whether he's stoned or not. The pot just makes them bigger, cooler, prettier.

His face is changing, has been changing. He smiles less than he used to, when he was still lively and alert, which already seems so long ago. And when a smile is there it's indecipherable. His eyes look inward. His expression is often blank, that strange, disconcerting flatness I've seen on our mother's face. I find myself picturing the brain behind that skull, trying to imagine what's happening in there, what's making his emotions slip away from his face. Sometimes his whole body is stiff, his spine almost like a board when he sits. When he stands, his arms hang straight down, palms inward. And when he moves, his gestures are too simple, too plain, too lacking the inflection of personality. It looks so obviously unnatural to me that I can't believe other people don't notice it. But they don't. Or they just think he's really stoned.

Melvin and I are outside a bar, closing time, and he buys a skewer of chicken from the man with the big grill at the edge of the road. It is warm and there is a light breeze that makes the tops of the dark palms shimmy beneath the stars.

"Pura carne," Melvin says to the man at the grill, smiling slyly. I'm standing a few feet away, not part of their conversation. He thinks he has pulled it off until we make eye contact and he realizes I was listening. He panics, leaping toward me, saying, "No, no! I meant *this*!" He's holding up his skewer. I nod and he knows I don't believe him, which is

fine, but he doesn't seem to grasp that I want to pretend I don't care.

He's waiting for me to say something. I just look at him. I do that now. I've stopped acknowledging that I have seen the things I have seen. I look at Melvin, how pretty he is, how little he knows about me, how hard he's trying to get me into his bed. Tom flits into my awareness and I blink him back out. I feel a profound sense of the pointlessness of reacting to anything.

I smile and step close to Melvin, and suddenly he pulls me in and takes my hand and begins to lead me up a gravel hill. The road is lined with bougainvillea that grows high over our heads. Near the ground their leaves are coated with dust, but up higher the branches swoop in grand arcs over and over themselves, and the flowers are hot pink and everywhere, and some part of me rolls away from my body and on into the bougainvillea, nesting there, tangling up in the greenery and the colors, holding tight to the vines, remaining behind as the body walks on toward the block of concrete that he says is home.

Another night I show up at a party and look for Melvin, hoping for a repeat encounter. He doesn't look for me, but once I find him he smiles and kisses me and wants to dance. I know sometimes at parties he doesn't want me there, but if I put myself in his way, he seems to decide *why not?* and then ends up taking me home. I'm dancing with the gringos I came with, in a group on the dance floor, drinking Cerveza Imperial. He comes and goes, bringing me beers, working the party and coming back to me between rounds. The gringos step aside to take a break and someone pulls out a joint. I'm aiming for the sweet spot I've discovered, working my way toward the right level of drunk/stoned that I can ride all night without crashing. I've been perfecting my approach, and I have this very finely tuned by now.

I don't try the cocaine. I don't really know why. I think I'm afraid of it. But more than that, I'm beginning to see the way it moves through the world. I am beginning to understand the symbolism of expensive white powder in a country whose people are mostly poor and mestizo. Melvin has started to tell me things. He points when the DJ ducks behind his turntables for a few minutes, music pumping on a brand-new song, then reappears. *"Cocaína,"* he says. He points out the crackheads, has known Mono since he was fourteen, says hello when he calls out to him, waves, shakes his head like he's a poor stupid fool.

The topic of my brother comes up and I say, "He's a genius." Melvin glances at me sidelong. He leans back slightly and looks me over and shakes his head.

I just watch. I notice when he steps behind the DJ booth. I see the communication by flicks of the eyes, with the guys who buy. Tan white guys a foot taller than him, cheerful to his übercool. Germans, Italians, Americans, Brits. The way he slips off to the side of the dance floor, places a cigarette in his mouth, reaches in his pocket for a lighter and then reaches farther, down past his long shorts to his sock, pulling up a small packet with his raised hand as he lights his smoke. He's smooth, makes everyone like him, acts like he's got their backs, speaking one of the languages he's taught himself, picked up on the beach and in bed with foreign girls. The young American guys are the most trusting—surfers from Bay Area bedroom communities. They think he's their pal.

I devour the look I see in Melvin's face as he chats them up, reaches to light their cigarettes and hands over his little packets, takes their money. He hates them more than I do. I can see this in his flashes of white teeth, his glistening eyes, and he knows I can see it and that's why he tells me things. He hates their money and the cluelessness it buys them and that they have so much more of it than he does, and for that I hate them even more because I know it means he hates me too.

Tom is getting worse, right before my eyes. I can't believe I'm actually watching it get worse. Hallucinations and blank expressions are taking over. The Tom I know is receding into a distant inner space. He doesn't ask where I go during the day, or at night. He doesn't see the fear on my face, the sadness in my eyes. One last time, I get angry at him—it's over nothing, nothing at all, but I cry like a girlfriend, upset by some offhand comment. He offers a baffled smile, says I'm making an awfully big deal out of it. It's like I have a volume knob and someone has turned it way down. He can still see the show, but he can't follow what it's about. This is the worst kind of betrayal.

I hold in some dark corner our lessons from childhood, from life with our mother, who never got help, never took meds, remained delusional for decades as her life slowly collapsed around her. Memories unfurl inside as I watch Tom. It is as if I already know that doctors and medications and hospitals and our efforts will all fail him. His personality is disappearing in front of me, and time has collapsed. I can't see beyond the edge of the day.

I say nothing directly. I can't bring it up. I ask a few questions, but I never say what I really think. Nothing could be more impossible. I can't stand here, in this dirty little town where people don't even speak my language, and tell Tom I think he has schizophrenia. I don't know what I would possibly do next. I don't know how I could live past that moment. I can't seem to understand that such a moment could occur and we could continue to exist beyond it. I arrive at the point of picturing myself saying, "I think you have schizophrenia," and then it all falls off the edge, like a ship on an ancient map.

Melvin's apartment is a large room on the second floor of a cube of concrete. The tin roof creaks above us, and mosquitoes get in through open vents near the ceiling. He has a bed in the corner, a TV on the shelf, and a dividing wall between apartments that rises to about four feet short of the high ceiling, so that when we make the bed bang against the outside wall, some neighbor with a middle-aged voice shouts at us to cut it out. Melvin hollers back, snarky, that he's almost there. I've never had sex before while knowing someone is listening. And I don't care, can't make myself care.

Afterward, as I watch him moving around the room, I have the thought that this is like I'm in a movie. It's not just the scene, its foreignness. It's a feeling that I'm not actually here. There is a glass between me and everything. There is glass inside me. Inside me something important and delicate has fallen and broken. Even when Melvin's talking to me, I'm in a separate universe that witnesses his but does not touch it.

He begins pulling things from his pockets and his shelves, setting them on a small, beat-up table. The packets of coke that were in his socks. A roll of cash. A scale. He sits down to do his work, scooping from a large bag into small bags on the scale, tying them off. I watch.

Melvin tells me things, mostly in English because he's noticed I have trouble following his Spanish. I'm embarrassed by this, but I let it be. Years ago I could speak Spanish well, but now when the words come into my head, they just sit there. The language won't move around in my mind. So Melvin sticks with English. His stories come out amid the rest of his chatter, random asides. His drunken father. Days without eating. Coming to Tamarindo as a teenager. One time, he cries. His mother, who left for New Jersey. Teaching himself Italian, English, German, trying to get out of here, always. He looks at me as if I'm a question in his head. "I don't know why I tell you so much," he says.

Tonight he pulls a pinch of tobacco from the end of his cigarette and replaces it with blow. I haven't known he does this. As he smokes he catches me watching him. A shadow, a child's shame, passes over his face. Then his eyes turn hard.

"Why you always look at me like that?" he says. "You look and look but you don't say nothing."

Another young Rasta who Tom befriends on the beach tells me a folktale about the ocean. He says there's a dragon that lives at the bottom of the sea, and it reaches out to touch every continent. I think about this story when I take walks past an old dead tree, fallen sideways, weatherworn and sinuous. I imagine the dragon's long limbs, twisting like DNA strands along the ocean floor, invisible, powerful.

Where does a mind go, when it is lost? When I look out to sea from the beach in Tamarindo I have a feeling, irrationally, that Tom is out there. I stare out across it, the impenetrable water, the sun-blasted water. I keep thinking that out there is where I last saw him, the Tom that I knew. I am thinking that he must be out there in the water, because if he's not there he's not anywhere.

Melvin disappears for a few days, and I know it's over. I hear from the woman who owns the motel, an American in her forties, that Melvin is a thief who steals from his *gringa* girl-friends. When he returns I find him outside a bar and ask him if it's true. I ask him if he was going to steal from me. He gets angry, takes me by the upper arm and pulls me under a street-light, saying, "I want to see your eyes." Searching my face, wanting to know why I would say that, why I would think he still does that kind of thing. Suddenly I realize he no longer has any need to steal—she must have had old information—and then I realize that's not the point anyway.

A girl he had his arm around in the bar waits for him several feet away. He's defending himself to me now—tells me about the men he works for, their guns. He tells me about a gun to his head, about stealing a car at gunpoint. He holds his two fingers up to my temple and stares me down, demanding with his eyes, with the pressure of his fingers against the bone of my forehead, that I understand what it feels like to be forced to steal a car at gunpoint.

And with those fingers at my temple, it is as if I can already see what will come, not for Melvin but for me. That several years later, after doctors and medications and our help have achieved little, after Tom has denied his illness and turned us away and landed in the soup kitchens and homeless shelters of downtown Anchorage, I'll know this beach is where I lost him. And that years in the future, at a beach again while on vaca-tion in Mexico, I'll find myself running frantically along the shore, alone, looking out past the breakers as they beat at my ankles, hollering, "Tom! Tom! Tom!" Looking for him, know-ing full well that he's nowhere near Mexico. I'll be sobbing as I run, and for several minutes I'll refuse to stop calling his name.

And I don't find a way to tell Melvin what I want to say. To say I am trying to unmake this, all of it. To say I'm paddling backward against the waves.

Gram Julia's Spies

I COME FROM A FAMILY OF STORYTELLERS. ON MY MOTHER'S side, storytelling is treated as an art form. Gesture, rhythm, and timing are all important, as are wit and lyricism. For my grandmother Barbara, storytelling was a way of inhabiting her own life and of creating a world for her family to inhabit. My mother, a gifted storyteller in her own right, spoke at length only of her elaborate delusions, almost never of life before she fell ill. But Barbara's stories spoke to me of my own life, of the *why* of things. They reached far back, to her Chicago childhood and further, through the generations. And it was in the cracks and crevices of those stories that I began to trace clues to our lineage of mental illness—a largely unacknowledged inheritance, often hushed or reconfigured, revealing itself obliquely.

There is the story of the Japanese spies. Told and retold by my aunts and uncles, a humorous tale about Barbara's mother Julia's high jinks, it goes like this: During World War II, when Chicago was on alert about a possible invasion, Gram Julia came to believe there were Japanese soldiers hiding in her walls. They had radios, she said, and they were spying on her family. She took to regularly calling the fire department and telling the firemen to come to her house and find these spies. The fire chief knew better than to listen to her and always found a way to avoid going out to the house. Until one night a substitute was in charge, and when Julia called he took her seriously. A fire truck arrived at the house and firemen commenced to hack apart a wall. When this revealed no spies, they left.

"She was a character," my aunts and uncles said of Gram Julia. She was bold and artistic, with interests in the paranormal and metaphysical. She had a powerful personality, very charismatic, and she could be a lot of fun. "Oh, you know," one aunt told me, "she always wore *red*." People were drawn to her. But she wasn't a nurturing type. She had a reputation for being selfish. She also believed she was psychic, and in 1932, when the Lindbergh baby was kidnapped, she became convinced that the child was nearby. She drove all through the streets of Chicago searching for him, thinking she could sense where he was, feel her way toward him, save the boy—when all the while, the baby was lying dead in the woods of New Jersey. The first time I asked Barbara what Julia was like, she opened her eyes wide and said, "No one else!"

Barbara was our family's master storyteller. A great lover of English novels, she had an instinct for timing and a flair for structural parallels, both honed by the literature degree she earned in midlife at UCLA. And the fact was I craved her stories and the past they revealed—back to the old family farm in southern Maryland, a onetime tobacco plantation called La Grange, where, in the late nineteenth century, Gram Julia was raised. Recalling that place and the summers she had spent there, Barbara's meandering words wound into our family tree like a spiral drill. It was through her stories that I felt her

My grandfather's favorite, it was a portrait of Barbara when she was young, statuesque and poised in a slim purple gown, with pale hands that slipped into the shadows of a bouquet of oversize blooms. And as the young Barbara gazed placidly out at us, her shoulders bare and lovely, the elderly Barbara would talk to me about whatever was on her mind. Sometimes this included even the sad stories, the stories of mental illness that she often refused to share with others. Those were her gift to me alone. For caring, I suppose. For asking. And more than that, for telling. She was like that—guarded, but ready to reciprocate what you offered.

Even in her nineties, Barbara was strangely, astoundingly, still beautiful. Her white hair. Her smile, fleeting and real. And sometimes when she turned, her gray-green eyes flashed in their deep sockets and the fine forms of her nose and cheek-bones shone, and there again was the face in the portrait. And as we sat beneath it I would begin to feel the canvas breathing her in and out, the flowers taking over. If I looked at it too long, her eyes grew so deep that I feared I'd fall in.

I was just beginning to understand that the distinction between mental health and mental illness is not always clear, in its broad terrain of indistinct and sometimes subjective markers. Schizophrenia's symptoms occur in many combinations and vary in intensity and frequency, highlighting how the complexities of the brain and the fuzzy boundaries of mental health can, and often do, give rise to variegated conditions. Today Gram Julia might have been diagnosed with schizophreniform disorder, a transient psychosis that resembles schizophrenia but is less debilitating. It is possible, too, that Julia's distorted perceptions were not disabling enough to constitute a disorder at all. After all, she managed all right without any treatment.

Whether she was genuinely disabled by her mental state is hard to know. She always had money and people to take care of her.

Julia's eccentricities do, however, seem a harbinger of what was to come. Her son Perry Jr., Barbara's brother, showed signs in adolescence of a mental health problem that soon developed into a serious, and mysterious, illness. It was something like schizophrenia but difficult to pinpoint. He had a major breakdown in early adulthood and spent several years in an institution—the famous Menninger Clinic. (Those were the days before the warehousing of the mentally ill was outlawed and America's asylums were emptied.) What's more, he was gay, at a time when homosexuality was considered a mental illness, and this was part of why he was sent to the clinic. Now this only muddies the picture I try to construct of his mental health. Perry was eventually released and moved into an apartment nearby, living the rest of his life within walking distance of the clinic, visiting his doctor every few days, holding no job, never quite able to live independently.

Barbara was told he had "manic depression"—bipolar disorder—though she said he showed no signs of the mood cycles that define that illness. "It was a catchall," she told me, handing over the information as if relieved to be freed of the burden of trying to make sense of it. Family descriptions of Perry's problems fit better within the schizophrenia spectrum—perhaps schizotypal personality disorder, which involves social indifference, withdrawal, and "unusual experiences of reality." Perry showed profound emotional detachment from others, as well as severe anxiety and, at times, crippling paranoia. He was friendly but solitary, disengaged, always unkempt. He never bought his furniture but rented it for decades. Nor would he open his mail, letting it pile up waist-high beside the door. His best friends were the stars of the movies he loved to watch. He may have been suicidal. And for a while at Menninger's he refused to leave his room, so certain was he that if he walked down the hall, a light fixture would fall onto his head.

Maybe all this helps explain some things about Barbara. For one, she never liked stories about talking animals—they made her uncomfortable. She disliked even the old nursery rhymes in which rabbits spoke to field mice. Once, when I made the mistake of renting the Peter Pan movie *Finding Neverland* for us to watch, she sat sullenly through the first half and then got up to go to bed. Other things that made her nervous included poems that didn't rhyme and novels that lacked a linear plot structure. Her favorites were Longfellow and Kipling, Jane Austen, Steinbeck. In conversations about modern fiction, she flatly denied she could follow a fragmented narrative, avowing that Toni Morrison's *Beloved* simply did not make sense to her.

I am told that she was deeply saddened by Perry's illness, by his failure to build any kind of life for himself and, more revealingly, by the way he never "fit in." It seems to me that all her life she believed that happiness would come to the well behaved. Hiding her anxieties behind a veneer of impatience, she was short-tempered with any action that upset what she took to be the natural order of things. Yet I always sensed, too, that some part of her strained against the very order she tried to impose. As if that tendency—compensatory, self-protective—was an inadequate solution and she knew it.

Yes, I know, I wanted to say sometimes. About the sense that no one but you was going to hang on to what was sensible, what was real. The conviction that any deviation into nonsense would lead to chaos, dissolution. The contempt, laced with terror, toward those who would be so cavalier with this thing called reality. As if reality were something you could simply cast off and live without. As if we don't absolutely need it, don't truly want it. As if that which is literal and measurable is not worth all our respect.

I was, for my part, having the stunning experience of finally understanding who I came from. In Barbara I found a relative I could recognize as a forebear to my own personality. I had always been sensitive and was beginning to see how moody I could be, how fierce my emotions run, how intense my tastes and desires. I had a sense that, in spite of myself, my life turned on absurdities and paradoxes.

How could I tell her that a fragmented narrative was the only kind that would ever do her justice? She would sometimes tell me how much she had liked the geometry class she took in high school, how she had done very well in the subject. How pleasantly straightforward it had been, with the lines and angles connecting, all the numbers adding up right. So logical, the way everything fit together. I understood that this anecdote communicated a deep wish, one we both knew had never been fulfilled.

In my family, psychotic illness has threaded its way through four generations in a row, from Gram Julia to Perry Jr. and then, via Barbara, to my mother and brother. And trickling around the clear cases of mental illness is something more diffuse—scatterings of our genetic susceptibility. There is no single schizophrenia gene. Rather, what we have inherited is a complex vulnerability in the form of a cocktail of mutations— hundreds or even thousands of rare alterations in genes that encode various brain proteins. Evidence suggests that none of these mutations are, by themselves, pathological—that only particular combinations lead to the emergence of the illness. But studies have shown that the children, siblings, and parents of people with schizophrenia often have abnormalities in brain structure and cognitive deficits that parallel, in lesser severity, those of their ill loved ones.

I catch glimpses of these traits in many of us. I've occasionally been blindsided by papers about such studies, recognizing in their dry descriptions some of my own quirks, like working memory impairments and difficulty identifying smells. One of my sisters says that when under a lot of stress, she sometimes hears voices. "Auditory hallucinations," she says. "I have them. Occasionally." She does not, however, believe that the voices are real. Nor do they interfere with her life. Still, when I think of this I feel my own luck wash over me like a cold wave. How close we have come.

Touched, my father says we are. Our family is what is called a multiplex family—one in which schizophrenia occurs in successive generations. Many of schizophrenia's underlying genes contribute to other disorders as well, and some aspects of the illness spectrum may additionally be linked to intelligence and creativity. Barbara had seven children, and among them and her twenty grandchildren I find the full range of this inheritance. Among my cousins, IQs are high and currents of creativity run thick, as do depression and anxiety, with a few addictions and some signs of mania, autism, and ADHD thrown in. We have had an architect, two lawyers, a chemical engineer, a radiologist, a Marine, a musician, a veterinarian, a massage therapist, and a professional psychic turned high school teacher. We are never boring.

It is a blend of nature and nurture that leads to the development of schizophrenia, a genetic susceptibility combined with environmental influences that begin shaping the brain just as it forms, in the womb. These may be chemical or social or physical and may occur throughout life—infections in utero, childhood trauma, cannabis use, et cetera. The potential causes are numerous and difficult to pin down. We can't predict who will get sick or why. And for reasons unknown to science, there is a trend in multiplex families toward increasing severity of illness in every generation. In ours this has held true.

I have had to wonder: What is the end point? Where does this lead? For direct offspring of people with schizophrenia, like my brother and sisters and me, the chances of developing the illness were around thirteen percent. For my niece and nephews, the chances are less—closer to five percent. Small enough if you've never had schizophrenia in your life, but for my sisters and me it would be our third time around, something it's hard to imagine facing. Considering having a child of my own, I used to wonder if it was worth the risk. But when I said so to other family members, some got angry, defiant. I get this. It feels like defeat to talk that way.

We have not long known how to speak about these things. Or even how to think about them. One evening when I was visiting Barbara for the weekend, as we sat watching television and chatting about my mother, she announced quite suddenly, "I think Mari is cured!" She smiled over at me. Caught off guard, I stared. My mother regularly regaled me with delusional narratives and was lately refusing to sign her name on all documents, no matter how important, because she believed a bank had stolen money from her account. Eventually I got out a reply—too blunt, too direct. "No," I said. A pause. "She's very delusional. And she's paranoid." In our eyes we saw that we were both stunned. I tried to soften my words, relaying a few things my mother had said to me recently as evidence. "Well," Barbara replied, her shoulders slumping as she turned her head away, "I guess she just doesn't tell me about all that."

I am told that Barbara believed my mother's illness was her own fault, either for passing to her daughter the damning genes or, as was once commonly believed, for having somehow been a cold and distant mother. I began to better understand this when she asked me, apropos of nothing, where in the body one finds one's genes. To never really see the bald truth of schizophrenia, though it surrounded her—to never grasp, even in a basic sense, what this thing was that was happening, always happening. Sitting with me at her kitchen table not long before she died, looking out the big window at her row of blooming roses, she told me, of her maiden name, "I used to think the Phelps line was Welsh. I thought that explained us. They say it's a Welsh trait to have the stormy personalities you see in our family." She paused. "Black moods . . . rage . . ." Her voice trailed off, as if she didn't know where to go next with her thought.

Sometime later, when I tried to discuss my brother with her, she launched into speculating about the ways new technology requires the young to always be thinking of "five things at once." I realized she was wondering if mental illness could be caused by the stress of multitasking. Then she asked, "Do you think he has schizophrenia, or do you think he just decided to live the way he wanted?" I started to explain, but my answer was too technical. I was confusing her. Then I couldn't tell if she was listening. Finally she said, with pressure in her words, "I guess I, I didn't want to know, probably, much about—and heaven knows we didn't know anything about the brain." She stared into the space in front of her as if trying to push it away with her eyes.

Where does this lead? It leads to more questions—about my sisters' children, my cousins' children. About treatment and the costs of treatment, about the difference between what works and what helps, about fear and optimism. It leads us to a future we can't see. And it leads, relentlessly, back to its precursor: Where have we been? We ourselves don't quite know. This is the way schizophrenia tangles things. It ruptures life stories, riddles history with unknowables. But it also points to how we continue on. I suspect that the only real weapon we in my family have ever had against mental illness is how we choose to live. We fight back by refusing to let existence be sapped of its beauty and its mystery and its joy.

One night, visiting Barbara after my grandfather passed away, I helped her to bed. She had by then rearranged the art to suit her own tastes, taking down the portrait of her younger self and replacing it with a Cubist still life. And over her bed, a solitary single bed in a room she now shared with no one, she had placed an eerie painting of an old-fashioned doll. It struck me every time I walked in the room. Unlike most of the art in the house, it was the sort of painting that could make people uncomfortable. Something about the angular composition, the dark gray background, the empty-eyed doll face touched here and there with electric, unnatural colors. It felt discordant, almost radioactive.

I was surprised that Barbara liked the painting. It seemed more like something I might own, with my weirder, darker tastes. But when I commented on it she said only, "I always thought she was such a lovely little thing." It was as if the image spoke to her of something in herself that she couldn't quite identify. Something she hadn't found the words for, and maybe didn't even know she wanted to say.

Asylum

IT WAS IN A LOS ANGELES SUBURB THAT I BOUGHT THE rainbow-striped capris and the sky-blue suede belt with stars punched out of it as if it were a night sky coming out in the daytime. I wore them with a tank top that was so pale pink it was nearly peach, the color of birth, of a newborn song. I had landed there, in Curran's apartment, after getting my brother out of Costa Rica—after convincing Dad that Tom had schizophrenia and seeing him as baffled as I was about what to do. I came dragging with me a cheap Panamanian guitar and a song I had written about Tamarindo. The song clashed in every way with the outfit—all minor chords and demands moaned out over the fret board. When I think of it now it has a visible form and it is black and it is red.

Curran didn't know what to do with me and neither did I. While she was at work I walked through her sprawled suburb, over traffic berms and across parking lots, to the nearby mall, where I purchased the colorful capris, the starburst belt. I spent days wandering the mall, looking at baubles in Claire's and sneakers in Payless—cheap stores selling cheap clothes, teenager clothes. Wandering was all I could think to do with myself, and that required having something to look at. And in Ventura County there was nothing to look at except at the mall.

Back in Curran's apartment, I looked at what I had found in the mirror. Trying on my new clothes, I experimented with eye makeup, applying pale greens and bright blues, blending the shades, adding thick mascara. Took myself in. Felt, there, that I was achieving something.

What is the difference between being seen and being heard? I played my guitar and sang while Curran napped behind a closed door, getting louder the longer she pretended to sleep through my noise. I actually wondered if she could hear me. I learned later that she was covering her head with a pillow so she could have a few more minutes of rest after another day of teaching special ed. How was I so oblivious? I don't think I knew that anyone could hear me, ever.

I have long believed I have a mild kind of synesthesia when it comes to music—songs have colors. David Bowie's "Ashes to Ashes" is lavender and blue-gray. His "Rebel Rebel" is orange and burgundy. U2's entire *Joshua Tree* album is royal blue and silver, while *Achtung Baby* is definitely indigo. These pairings are vague and inconsistent enough, though, that I'm not sure if it is synesthesia or simply my wildly associative mind at play. Maybe I just extracted those colors from videos and album covers and lyrics and my own moments of being with those songs, culled them from the slurry of my memory in forming the qualia that give things their meanings.

White noise, people say. *Loud colors.* Using color to describe audio, or volume to stand in for brightness. Conflating sound and vision, identifying some truth about the way being heard *is* being seen. The way articulating one's thoughts makes one visible.

Curran told me I could stay as long as I liked, leave whenever I wanted. But I knew I was impossible. I didn't stay long. Next, I landed in Bozeman, only because I had lived there before, a ski bum. Only because I couldn't think of anywhere better to go. My friend Tasha suggested I get a job at the bakery where she worked and where I had worked the previous winter, as a barista and driver of an ancient yellow delivery van. She thought I should come back and learn how to bake, so I did. This was good, to be kneading dough and mixing batter from early morning until midafternoon. Something to do with my hands, to keep my body occupied while my mind wandered, got lost, found itself again. And to be not alone but listening to the others talking and laughing and kidding around, pulling me out of myself enough that I could relax a little. Because in my time off, the fact of schizophrenia swept over me and held me under. I kept having moments in which I would look around and feel that nothing I saw was actually there. Or conversely, that all was as usual and I myself did not exist. Some sense of connectivity between self and environment, spirit and form, had been severed. And the more time I spent with nothing to do, the worse it got.

The clothes, the mounting hours spent in front of the mirror, somehow helped. I picked up a couple of tubs of Manic Panic and hunted down some old-school hair bleach from a beauty supply store and started streaking my long wavy hair. First I bleached strips all around my head and then I dyed some of them turquoise and some of them pink and some of them burgundy. I kept my long bangs back with glittery clips in orange, turquoise, and pale green, and bobby pins with rhinestones on them. I added eye shadow in every color, shimmery, iridescent, shot through with glitter.

On days off, I went to the Gallatin Valley Mall. I spent time in Bon Marché and Hot Topic and Rue21. I bought a bright yellow shirt emblazoned with an antique ad for peaches, a red peacoat with enormous buttons down the front, a sky-blue T-shirt with a stylized beach scene of palm trees and sunset, trimmed with scarlet at the collar and sleeves. I bought pinstriped jeans and white bell-bottomed corduroys with blue stripes in various widths. I was aware that I was too old for this and also aware that I did not care.

I stood out, in Bozeman, in color and sparkle. I had never worn dramatic clothes much before. Anchorage had been like the rest of the Pacific Northwest, all grunge and granola. And I had gone to college in Oregon at the height of Pearl Jam's moment—I was in love with Eddie Vedder and I dressed like him too. Levi's 501s and oversize T-shirts, short-sleeved over long-sleeved. Doc Martens, Vans, plaid flannel. Dark colors— forest green, navy. That evolved, back in Alaska and then Montana, into a wardrobe of outdoor wear. Leather hiking boots and fleece pullovers, sunglasses with polarized lenses.

Boyish clothes, I felt, were better than girlish clothes. I was obsessed with appealing to boys and found the pressure so intense that refusing to dress as if I were obsessed with appealing to boys was my only recourse. It took away the edge, the intensity of my desire to be desirable. I thought attraction was about approval. I thought I was looking for someone who would approve of me. And, secretly, I was angry that this would be the case and probably rebelling against it just as I strived for it. None of this was conscious, of course. I lived in an ongoing state of not-knowing. For the first decade of my adulthood I managed to not-know myself at all. Then I tried to not-know that my brother had schizophrenia and I collapsed.

Almost. Not a complete collapse but perhaps a scattering.

I tried on my clothes and stared at myself, changed outfits, stared at myself some more. Put on some eye makeup, looked again. From the Buffalo Exchange next door to the bakery I got a pair of red boot-cut pants and some pale blue bell-bottomed jeans, and a tan suede A-line miniskirt that did everything for my legs. In a boutique downtown, I found a black suede jacket with faux-fur trim at a steep discount. What I couldn't find, I made. On a plain black T-shirt I painted, in glittery orange puff paint, THE MATRIX IS REAL. As if I needed to make myself more visible to counter this feeling of unreality. As if I might dissolve right out of existence, were it not for the stripes, the sparkles—my own image reflected back at me—holding me in place.

I had a look going within a couple months, punctuated by the piles of jewelry I tossed on to complete the outfits. Rings with enormous faux gemstones, bangle bracelets by the dozen. My neck was busy with silver chains, one dangling with a pendant of Saint Christopher that my mother had given me. I had a cross from her, too, inset with gems of blue and yellow and pink and red. I didn't exactly believe in God, but I did believe in my mother's love and that seemed a good enough reason to wear them.

Eventually I found my way to the color that is not a color. I bought a flared black skirt embroidered with thin flowers and wore it sometimes to create a kind of goth Opposite Day, pairing the skirt with a black sweater and thick-heeled boots and heavy eyeliner. I would sit reading in the coffee shop, feeling as though I was announcing something to the world. And I was pleased when my two punk friends spotted me and came over grinning, saying I looked great. But then the next day I could not carry on the blackness. It was overwhelming in its pessimism, too bleak a portrait of the place where I held the fact of schizophrenia. I would spring back to rainbows, colors, stars, sunsets, palm trees, bright skies.

I don't know how I came up with the idea to dress the way I did. It just happened. There was something of the tropics in it, of Tamarindo and Tom's bright visions. There were also memories of childhood, of Jem and the Holograms and maybe Willy Wonka too. And a dose of the archetypal rock star, the person who writhes and wails onstage, who worships things and then smashes them. I had once had that poster of Jimi Hendrix in which he kneels, in a ruffled yellow blouse, over the guitar he has set on fire. But mostly, I think, it was about disintegration. I felt as though Tom's illness had pushed me through a sieve—or, more appealingly, through a prism that refracted all my wavelengths, rendering me as rainbows.

I talked about Tom only rarely. I didn't know much about what was going on with him because I couldn't stand to think about it. And yet on some level it was all I thought about, a background noise that I couldn't turn off. I did sometimes say, "I think my brother has schizophrenia." To close friends, a few friends. But no one grasped what the illness was, really, or what it meant to my family. And I didn't have it in me to explain.

Within a few months, Dad convinced Tom to leave Boulder and move back to Anchorage, so he drove up in the new SUV he had bought with day-trading money and got an apartment. He looked for work, but nothing took shape. Dad told him he believed he was having mental health problems and pressed him to see a doctor, or even a counselor, even a minister. But Tom refused. He did admit that in the past he had gotten his hands on some Trilafon, an antipsychotic that is rarely prescribed anymore, and that it had helped clear his thinking. But he didn't want to go see anyone about getting a prescription, for that or anything else. Dad, frustrated, ended up uselessly lecturing him on the need to get his shit together.

Tom didn't do much more each day than live inside his own head. That summer when Dad, wanting to give him a way to earn some money, asked him to mow his lawn, he later found him standing out there on the grass, the lawnmower running while he stared off into space. When I called Tom, he talked seriously of becoming a professional soccer player and said he spent many hours training. I asked what that entailed and he explained that it was not physical training but visualization. He added that he was still deciding whether he should become a soccer player or a superhero.

I didn't bother, really, to wonder why Tom refused to go to a doctor. It was what Mom had always done, for no reason apparent to anyone. Some mix of denial and incapacitation, of illness and stubbornness. I knew that one aspect of psychosis is that its workings often render sufferers unable to grasp that they are in an altered state—*impaired insight,* doctors say—but the boundaries of insight are vague, its definition hazy. It involves personality as well as pathology. Tom felt a sharp sense of failure beneath the bright light of his psychosis, a truth that was hard for him to face. And it likely also had to do with the particular nature of his symptoms: grandiose, rapturous. "Mental illness can be very seductive," my friend Sean told me, thinking of his own bipolar disorder. These were choices made at the confluence of circumstance and biology, pride and shame, fortitude and fear.

.   .   .

"Don't you wonder sometimes about sound and vision?" sang David Bowie on the album *Low*. That standing back from perception, finding the seams in its illusory seamlessness, questioning things usually taken for granted—it requires a breakdown of sorts, a disruption of the brain's efficient systems, of its usual tracks of sensation and thought, long enough to see beyond them. When I hear this song, I think about how witnessing schizophrenia up close tends to make people curious about the contours of reality.

The story I thought I knew about Bowie was the one everyone told: He was *glam*—fabulous, flashy. I believed this until I began looking closely at footage and images from the era of Ziggy Stardust and Aladdin Sane, and I was struck that Bowie's costumes seemed oddly less about glitz than something much more bizarre, much more random. He wore what looked like a Japanese kimono restyled almost as a women's bathing suit. He performed in a turquoise feather boa and a one-legged unitard, or a bodysuit that appeared to have been crocheted by hand. He posed in a leisure suit of quilted material that looked like it might have been pulled from his parents' bed. He paired cherry-red patent leather boots with a jumpsuit cut from drab upholstery fabric. The look's power came less from its flash than from its disjunctions, its appearance of having been reconstituted from scraps. It was as homespun as it was dramatic, the juxtapositions jarring, the textures often homely. It was at times incoherent, pulled together by no clear organizing principle. Bowie later described it as "a cross between Nijinsky and Woolworths." It was, as a friend of his once said, "a spectacle of not-belonging."

Creativity shares some things in common with mental illness. For example, in order to arrange diverse ideas into something original, something new, the mind must first deconstruct its existing order. It must free itself from preconceptions and pursue alternate possibilities. The brain's "default" state, a restful mode that occurs, for instance, when people daydream, allows for this by activating networks that enable communication among disparate regions of the brain, linking ideas that would usually not be connected. During these periods of associative, speculative, wandering thought, the mind becomes temporarily disorganized, freed from the demands of reality. The artist's task is to then piece things back together in fresh and revealing ways.

The chaos that occurs when thoughts associate freely is to me a great friend and a great danger. The process is unconscious, beyond my control, and it is similar to what occurs in depression, mania, and psychosis. And truly, when my associative mind is in full swing, nothing else quite functions right. Conversation gets difficult. Paying bills is confusing, buying groceries a challenge. I catch myself thinking out loud, sometimes in public. Yet these are the times when I have come out with paintings, poems, chord progressions, lyrics, stories, prints, costumes, essays.

I wasn't inspired by David Bowie so much as I walked into him backward. I didn't know much at all about who he was or what he created, aside from his radio songs. But what I came to appreciate about him much later, what I related to as I learned and listened and grew to be a fan, was his beautiful disjointedness. His art was carnivorous, devouring influences and spitting them out scrambled, shaped by his history and diverse fascinations. His suburban upbringing, 1960s London, art school as a would-be painter, various creative forms—French mime, Kabuki theater, Beat poetry, German Expressionist cinema—and a family history riddled with schizophrenia.

The illness ran on his mother's side. Three of her siblings spent time in institutions, two of them with schizophrenia diagnoses. There had been electroshock therapy, depression, a lobotomy, and his mother was unstable as well. So mental illness was a kind of background noise for Bowie and his half brother, Terry, his protector and role model. A decade older, Terry introduced him to most of his early influences, like jazz and sci-fi and Buddhism. But as Bowie grew up, Terry, too, started to show signs of schizophrenia. Bowie first saw it at the age of twenty, one night walking home after a Cream concert, when Terry was overtaken by a violent hallucination. "He saw the roads opening up, fire in the cracks in the roads," Bowie later recalled, describing how Terry went down on all fours, clinging to the pavement, saying he was being sucked up into the sky. "I had never seen anybody in that kind of metaphysical change before, and it scared me an awful lot."

Terry was institutionalized, and a few years later his illness became a central theme in Bowie's album *The Man Who Sold the World*. Its first cover bore a drawing of Cane Hill Asylum, where Terry lived, while the song "All the Madmen" considered the physical and emotional isolation of asylum residents. Even *The Rise and Fall of Ziggy Stardust* in many ways dealt with questions about schizophrenia and its consequences—alienation, a sense of doom. Ziggy and the other alter egos Bowie created, he later explained, were meant to protect him from insanity, becoming vessels for the madness he feared, keeping it at a safe distance. Yet the boundaries between self and character easily blurred. He later said, "I was so lost in Ziggy. It was all the schizophrenia. And it just got to be too much." I don't know exactly what he meant by this, but it is revealing that he chose that word to explain what happened.

References to schizophrenia threaded through later albums as well, not least of which was 1973's *Aladdin Sane*—a homophone for "a lad insane"—the persona that bore the now iconic red and blue lightning bolt makeup. "It was schizophrenic," Bowie said of the *Aladdin Sane* album. He apparently meant this in the slang sense, the *split mind* sense that does not accurately describe the illness, but there is his preoccupation, persisting. It also suggests the actual schizophrenic man who was always on his mind. And how it felt to lose so much to madness. There is the way the lightning bolt shoots across his face on the album cover. All the schizophrenia. Something about being struck apart.

I didn't think much about why I created a new look of my own, one that was, if not outlandish, then certainly eye-catching. I knew only that it felt deeply, pressingly necessary. Meandering through the racks at Buffalo Exchange, hunting for bargains after work, I found a small mesh shirt, navy blue and lavender, screen-printed across the front with the word ASYLUM. It pulled at me like a magnet. It suggested mental illness, of course, and old ideas about what it was and what to do with it. Institutions with echoing halls and blank-eyed sufferers shuffling aimlessly. But I also thought of safety, refuge, shelter. Which was a relief, really, to consider—that the word was supposed to mean something good. And there was this: To display it on my body felt like a transgression.

It called to mind one afternoon the previous winter when I was manning the bakery counter. It was slow, the loaves baked and the rush over, and I was alone with the coffee machines and trays of sweets when I heard the noise of many voices and looked across the street to see a small crowd of people walking by, holding up signs and chanting. I went to the window and caught the words *mental illness* on a couple of the signs. Saw a name: National Alliance on Mental Illness. I stared, listening—shouts and responses calling for support, visibility, awareness. *My God,* I thought, gaping. *Someone gives a fuck.*

I wore the *asylum* shirt to work, threw a soft white apron over it, rolled out cinnamon roll dough in it. People noticed it, commented on it during our daily chatter. It became synonymous with me, with whatever it was that made me interesting to my friends. Over a series of mornings, we collectively decided that Tasha would someday open a bar called the Asylum and I would perform there occasionally on electric guitar, on a little stage not unlike the one we flocked to on Thursday nights to sing karaoke. This was where I first understood that you could find asylum in exposure.

When I look back on that time, I want to say that what happened was everything. Everything happened. That was the year I took my first creative writing class. That was the year I stopped going back to Alaska. That was the year I found my way to a therapist who asked me about my life, and I started to tell her, and then I went home and nearly puked in the toilet. It felt awful but it also felt good, so I kept going back, talking ever-tightening circles around the fact of schizophrenia. I appeared in her office in the *asylum* shirt. I appeared in her office in yellow, blue, pink, white, red. I appeared in her office.

By the time Bowie wrote "Sound and Vision," in 1976, he was in Berlin, cloistered away in a small apartment in an attempt to kick a raging coke habit. He had by then had his share of delusions and paranoia himself—severe "cocaine psychosis" brought on by the drug, the kind of thing that led him to believe he was controlling the TV with his mind and that witches were stealing his sperm. Surely his brother's illness and confinement were part of what Bowie was escaping by staying high. Perhaps, too, there was a fatal kind of loyalty at play, a wish to explore madness for his brother's sake. Or maybe it was more like inertia, succumbing to the belief that his own loss of sanity was inexorable.

I wondered often about reality. About the difference between the physical universe and the universe as our human minds construct it. Red, for instance—something our brains make for us. Beyond us, outside of us, it is light at a wavelength of about 680 nanometers, photons moving up and down at a particular rate as they travel. The point being that we're never in direct contact with reality. And also that some ways of being wrong are useful, while others are not. It is mental illness only when the wrongness makes it harder to survive rather than easier.

I wondered about words too, more and more all the time. The ways I could arrange them on the page. The ways others arranged them. Including Tom, his words now scrambled by schizophrenia, in a screed he wrote not long before we went to Costa Rica. He had sat down in the dining room one day and opened my new laptop to take a look, and then typed out a couple of pages in a brief burst: "The Greatest Story Ever Qritten . . ." I found it in a folder some time later and kept the file among my own random writings, occasionally pulling it up to read, trying to decipher it as one would a message in a bottle.

It was a dizzying document, mythic and strangely compelling, though barely comprehensible—words combined, collapsed, rearranged, broken down into sounds, full of assonance and alliteration and errors allowed to stand.

. . . Now blisten dere's in de tributrees a worbloed distinct to brlassted reflecsurrection to ours . . . Long ago freminin seed there could angods feel breathe, though knouw into devil's light darkness we've all fallen. . . . From this salsizar the reemer entered throguth, and yeah we wond what is this sound . . . I tell the it is a harlequin mask of do. . . . Yet when and win tee ten he on to brice did roll, though leauty, loy, and love evanscerate against the imgoodrant, ignorant tide, still agast the ghrend he walked . . .

Reflecsurrection. Evanscerate. Agast the ghrend. I read it out loud sometimes, searching in the sounds of the words for some clue to make the tantalizing flashes of meaning cohere. It felt oracular, almost, as if embedded in it I could find the future, what to do.

.   .   .

As the months passed, the shadow on my lids grew more metallic and my eyeliner got thicker, blacker. I blended liner into shadow in a deep, shimmery charcoal and plenty of mascara. This reached its peak on a trip home to Anchorage in the fall, where, seeing Tom in essentially the same condition as before, I wore my eye makeup thick and dark every day. It was so glaring that Tom felt the need to comment on it. He said, "Marin, you're wearing way too much eye makeup."

But I couldn't not wear it that way. It was at once my armor and my leakage through the armor, the leakage of things I could no longer shunt aside and no longer wanted to. I wanted it to be the first thing anyone saw, especially people who already knew me. I wanted to surprise and confuse them, to shake them up enough to question what they thought they saw in me. It was suddenly necessary to project the thing I had always kept secret: *I am not the person you think I am.*

I was glad to be with Tom for a few days, connecting in our way, but I also felt as if we were choking in some kind of toxic, slow-burning fog. As if I were reaching for him through it and only half finding him. As we sat on the carpeted floor of his apartment, picking vaguely at his guitars among his empty beer bottles and open cereal boxes, he told me he had discovered that he had sprouted crystalline wings. He could feel them growing from his shoulder blades. They shimmered and glowed and grew bigger all the time, expanding as his own consciousness expanded. He spoke, in rhapsodic tones, of the time his body turned into liquid diamonds—his tissues flowing in faceted brilliance, inside and out.

He was nearly out of money by then and had already sold his SUV. He wrote a letter to our grandmother asking for financial support. A few months later, she showed me the letter. It described his recent experiences and said that he would be "very very very very very very very very very very very" grateful to have some extra funds. He explained, "I have come to realize that most people can't see their wings."

What was I doing with all those colors? All that flair? That spectacle of not-belonging.

I didn't know anything about Bowie's family until much later, after he died, when I became momentarily obsessed by his visual artistry and pursued it all the way back to schizophrenia. I kept asking myself, *How did I know?* I was reading that, in 1985, Terry climbed over the wall of the psychiatric hospital where he lived and lay down on some railroad tracks, letting a London express train plow over him. I was reading that, by then, Bowie had given up drugs for good when he gained custody of his son and became a single father. I was thinking about how he rescued himself, not once but over and over until he didn't have to anymore.

It was almost too eerie. Or maybe it wasn't. Maybe it was just exactly right, in the way influence can feel perfect and inevitable. Kind of like Halloween of that year in Bozeman, when I went to my friends' party dressed as Marilyn Manson. I didn't listen to Manson's music, but I liked his look as a costume, so I painted a black stripe across my face and put on a black wig and platform boots and a blue-tinted contact lens that I had ordered online. At the time, I didn't know that Manson's aesthetic was a dark descendant of Bowie's, that it was from Bowie that he borrowed the mismatched eyes, that his getup often directly referenced Bowie's personas—alien, feminized, extreme. Incidentally, I had expected my contact lens to turn my eye a glacial blue, as Manson's was, but the lens was not opaque and so instead the effect was as if I had, like Bowie, one enormously dilated pupil.

And as it happened, my friend Angie showed up at the party in a lavender spandex unitard, her face painted with the famous lightning bolt. "I'm David Bowie's Biggest Fan!" she announced, bouncing gleefully. Not long after, our friend Tim came down the stairs dressed up as *me*. I laughed out loud. He wore a wig of blond- and blue- and pink-streaked hair, clipped everywhere with barrettes, along with a mess of bright necklaces, a pair of striped, multicolored bell-bottoms, and my *asylum* shirt, which he had borrowed through subterfuge and squeezed over a pair of balloon breasts. Together we formed a wacky triangle: Angie as some girl dressed up as Bowie as Aladdin Sane, me as Marilyn Manson's dark reimagining of

Bowie's aesthetic, and Tim as me being my own thing, which turned out to be deeply Bowie-esque. All of which, in some sense, owed its existence to schizophrenia.

I think I was trying to do what Bowie had done—to find a way to continue on in the presence of schizophrenia. I think the art making, the songwriting, the wild, colorful displays became means to draw from the illness some of its potency but not its poison. I think I was beginning to see my wings.

Disintegration, Loops

.

LOOP: 2001/1991

IN SEPTEMBER OF MY SECOND SUMMER IN TOK, IN THE SUB-arctic black-spruce bogs of Alaska's interior, I awoke at about 4:30 each morning and spent the next six hours up on a small hill, catching songbirds. In nearly invisible mist nets our research team caught them as they flew through the forest, where they stopped to eat and sleep during their long flight south. Yellow-rumped warblers, dark-eyed juncos, Swainson's thrushes—doing my rounds from net to net, I plucked them loose and carried them in cotton bags back to the tent, where we would band them, measure them, take notes about their plumage, and then set them free. It was late morning when we rode the Fish & Wildlife Suburban back into town and passed the post office, where I noticed that the flag was flying at half-mast and wondered why.

I was twenty-six and Tom was not yet ill and the world, to me, was still more or less a forest beneath the wide ether, the home country of the sharp-eyed kinglets and sparrows and crossbills I saw each day. In the big back room at the headquarters building, our crew leader met us in the doorway and said, "The World Trade Center has been hit by a plane." His eyes were wide with excitement. "Both towers collapsed!" My mind turned over and came up empty.

He showed us the footage on his computer monitor—that clip of the second plane disappearing as a smoking pair of rectangles seemed to eat it up. I don't remember being upset. I was stunned, yes, and riveted, and I do think I was horrified. But even after we returned to the bunkhouse and turned on the television, after we spent the next two hours watching the same footage and piecing together the news accounts of the four planes, the crashes, the suicides, the rescues, the rest . . . it didn't sink in like it was supposed to.

Like it was supposed to. Now this phrase seems to contain everything I knew and felt and wondered during those years. My utter failure to react. The whole country was in a state of alarm, and I wanted to feel like I was part of that, like my home and my way of life had been attacked. But I didn't.

I was young and from a state with fewer than a million people and national parks larger than Rhode Island. And though I had traveled outside the country and all around the West, I had only rarely, briefly, been east of the Rockies. My way of life, as far as I knew, looked nothing like that of those New Yorkers who I imagined spent their days fifty stories above the earth, their eyes on computer screens and telephones at their ears. It was a city I had only once seen and never understood, on the other side of the continent, in a culture that was purportedly my own but to which I had always, as an Alaskan, felt like an outsider. My life, as I saw it, was about holding small birds in my hands.

Most of us at Fish & Wildlife were not radical in our thinking. We were liberal and countercultural, but in the end we were politically moderate. In the weeks after the attacks we were subdued except for my crew leader, who went on about how America should have seen this coming and that of course we deserved this. I didn't like his misanthropy—he had once said in all seriousness that he would rather rid the planet of automobiles than have world peace—but truly, his detachment from the horror of that day wasn't so different from mine. On television I saw crowds of thousands gathering in collective grief. They were in places I couldn't even picture—New Jersey, Iowa, Pennsylvania—and they seemed to feel a bond with New York that I couldn't comprehend.

But maybe what explains things better is that I had already had one catastrophe in my life. I was out there in the woods with my little songbirds, trying to hide from the very close, very personal fallout of the much more human-size disaster that was my mother's illness, her long decline, her impending poverty. I couldn't, did not want to, feel that this bigger disaster was mine to mourn. Now it seems that 9/11, for me, was never what it was, but had meaning only as a stand-in for other things in my life that I shared with almost no one.

Two thousand one—that was the summer my housemate Abby totaled my Subaru station wagon on a drive down to Haines as I sat in the passenger seat beside her. I had in previous months begun to write out a few scraps about my life with my mother. My ferocious memories, raw on the page. Abby had read them and praised them. But I had no idea what to do with them next. They resisted any structure I tried to give them.

Abby was only twenty-two or so and was not Alaskan and had never been on that highway, a shoulderless strip that wound along the Chilkat River through its narrow valley into town. We were coming in from the north just as dusk began to fall, and since it was August, it was the first time we had seen dusk since May. On the far side of the river a chaotic ridge rose, touched with late light on the white of snowfields at all angles. I was pointing out the peaks when I looked back at the road and saw a moose casually crossing our path.

A wasted eon passed as I waited for Abby to react, realized she didn't see it, and willed my lips to speak: "Moose." It felt like a whisper, and already irrelevant. The moose was a large female trailed by a small calf, and she was just entering our lane.

"What?" Abby said. She was still glancing at the mountains. By the time she dropped her foot hard on the brake, the animal was so near that all I could do, as the front bumper touched her foreleg and swept it out from under her, was close my eyes. I saw the dark mass of her hindquarters floating toward me, then sightlessly felt a tinkling rain of shattered glass touch the right side of my face. The moose rolled up over the hood and smashed in the right corner of the steel frame, cobwebbing my half of the windshield and blowing the side window in on me before our momentum lifted her up over the top of the car.

If I go back another decade, to around 1991, I find myself in a peach-colored duplex on a woody Anchorage cul-de-sac. My mother's house. There are the pinks and beiges of her decor, the chocolate smell of her cupcakes. She keeps finches these days, my teenage years.

It has been a good five years now since she succumbed to mental illness, and we have settled into what I will someday refer to as the *new normal*. Life is an intimate dance with insanity. My mother's delusions are wild and I hate to listen to them. Her fascinations are confounding, her behavior nonsensical. Her body has fallen into neglect and her life tilts sideways, ever in response to misapprehended cues. She still manages her house, but she inhabits another realm, one I can neither visit nor envision. From that distant place she encounters the rest of us, poorly translated. She is abstractly loving and brutally blind.

And this is what sticks:

The cat has killed the birds again. In their cage they were captives to Sweetie's swatting paws and staring eyes, flitting about to avoid her claws, perching sideways on the vertical bars, back and forth across the space to keep away. This, unless my mother was loading them into her car and driving off with them repeatedly to Girdwood, the little ski town where she bought a condo after the divorce and now visits as often as possible, for reasons I can't discern. Birds, I have learned, handle neither cats nor car rides well. Now our delicately striped zebra finches, a mating pair, are dead from the sheer stress of it all. I have watched as they slowly lost their soft feathers and grew bare in anxious agony, revealing patches of gray skin along their necks and backs before collapsing and dying. This has happened before, and each time my mother just buys more. She somehow doesn't see what she is doing. The cat. The driving. I try to tell her, I shout and stomp, but it doesn't help. She assures me that the birds are just fine, they are happy, they are okay. She keeps replacing them and I keep watching them die.

After the impact of the crash I opened my eyes to find the corner of my car's steel frame just above my right brow, at least half a foot beneath its usual position. Abby pulled over, and when we got out I hopped around on the shoulder a few times as the glass fell inside my jeans. I unzipped them to clear the slivers out of my underwear, and when we looked back we saw the moose lying behind us in our lane, struggling to stand on her broken legs. I turned away fast, but the image of the creature rising slightly and then collapsing, rising again and falling, vibrated through my mind. Abby and I stared at each other for a moment. Bizarrely, neither of us was hurt. Not even a scratch from all those shards.

Abby didn't understand what would happen to the moose now. She wanted to know if we could help it.

"Its legs are broken," I said. "God, I hope someone comes along and shoots it."

"Where's the calf?" she asked.

"The calf's gone," I said. "The calf will die."

"Why? Maybe it will be okay."

I felt a flash of irritation. "It ran into those bushes, by the river," I said. "There are bears down there. It won't survive."

She tried to argue the point. "No," I said, trying to be patient. "All the bears are gathered by the river now, because the salmon are running. Wolves are down there right now too. Without its mother, it won't live."

Later I would replay in my mind that conversation, and the moment of the crash—the moose's heavy body in the field of air before me, no time to move anything but my eyelids, the bits of glass brushing my face. Finding the ceiling compressed halfway down to my fragile forehead. There was even something magical about the way the glass had sparkled on my clothes, the sound it made when I shook it off onto the road. But it would be another decade before I understood how much I identified with the calf.

"Of course loss is the great lesson," Mary Oliver once wrote, and I taped it on my wall. By my mid-twenties I was drowning in that lesson, trying and failing to escape the fact of that lesson when I rode into town after a morning of bird banding and saw the flag flying at half-mast. After absorbing the looped footage of the falling towers and listening to clips of citizens' dismay, I began to feel a bit nonplussed, offended, even outraged to see all of America so shocked by the fact of this loss.

I had only a vague feeling that I should have cared more about the deaths and survivors than I did. On the news, college students spoke of "the end of innocence." America, it seemed, had collectively fallen into a state of blind contentment in the 1990s and now was being snapped out of it. *Whose innocence?* I kept thinking. *Shouldn't they already know all this? Shouldn't they know that it all can disappear?*

The primary emotions I felt in reaction to 9/11—or more specifically, to America's collective reaction to 9/11—were contempt and envy. I was jealous that someone had been innocent, and full of contempt that they had believed they could stay that way.

LOOP: 2011/2001/1987

I have always thought of nostalgia as something to avoid. I suppose that after a decade of relying on my wits to discern reality from within the clouds of my mother's delusions, I distrusted that rosy glow. I was more prone to pure forgetting—a protective, shielding kind of forgetting that just let the gaps lie. Now they attest, however blindly, to pains once felt, things lost, small horrors witnessed, moments not seized, days gone awry.

I can identify the beginning of this forgetting as my twelfth year, the year I faced and could not comprehend the odd half loss of my mother to mental illness. Sometimes it seemed her whole soul had collapsed. That the person we knew had been replaced by a stranger. Yet the stranger knew our mother, had known our mother. The stranger vaguely acknowledged her, sometimes seemed quite like her, maybe occasionally *was* her. And the body, the body rolled on, insistently present. The face I recognized. The eyes, the hands, the hair—it was all still there. Still moving, inhabiting space, showing her age.

My tactic was to resist the incomprehensible by shedding it immediately. And it was easy to do. Outside my mother's house, life continued as usual. Others rarely spoke of her, or to her, and when they did they usually behaved as if she was just fine.

By the year of 9/11, my gaps were taking over. They not only pocked the past but also riddled the present with holes. Spaces left by all my forgettings, growing wider with age, were becoming too obvious to ignore. I rarely spoke about my mother and I was beginning to see that ever larger chunks of my life were falling into the void of that non-telling. Half of my childhood, more. Whatever mechanism enabled me to forget a moment so easily required that I not really be present as the moment was happening. This had become habit, my usual mode of facing anything uncomfortable or sad: shut down, do not absorb. Habitual now was the muffled safety of non-presence, as were the hundreds of hours I spent alone in the woods in self-imposed isolation.

Even as I tried to write my scraps, I was noticing I had certain habits of storytelling that troubled me. I created gaps. I heard myself sometimes, telling the story of the crash with the moose with zest, evoking the high drama, yet I was aware that I was not saying what felt most important to remember. The image of the moose in the road, unaware that she was crippled, was its searing centerpiece. But I always left out the part about her calf.

Will and I found ourselves living in New York in the fall of 2011. It was early in our relationship, not long after we both moved there from Santa Fe, when I went to study writing and some months later he followed to join me. Will had lived in New York before, and we talked about our contrasting memories of 9/11, off and on, for weeks as the date of the tenth anniversary approached. He had been in Brooklyn on the day the planes flew into the towers. That was long before I knew him, when he was married to someone else and had a little girl, and a boy just days away from being born. He stood on his Cobble Hill rooftop and watched the first tower smoking. He felt the stages of surprise that I never experienced: first, the assumption that the first plane was also the last. Then the greater shock when a second plane appeared seventeen minutes later. And again when the towers began to collapse. He smelled the odor of burning debris that filled the city. He watched the bits of paper that floated on the air, blown across the East River from a hundred stories high. A scrap landed on the roof beside him. "Mom," it said, and a phone number.

As the anniversary came nearer, Will recounted the ardor of his protectiveness toward his new son, who was born on the twentieth, and how he and his then wife stopped fighting for nearly two months. He mentioned the day an envelope filled with anthrax was mailed to an office not far from the midtown building where he worked. When I Googled the anthrax attacks of 2001, I was stunned to learn that five people had died. I never knew.

I asked him to mark the day with me, saying I wanted to visit Ground Zero and see the crowds, the New Yorkers. I felt that maybe this time I could touch what happened in a way I had never managed to before. I felt embarrassed by my younger self. I wanted to confront 9/11, to feel a connection with the people who lived it, as I had so fully failed to do in 2001.

Will agreed, somewhat neutrally. This was his first September back in the city after several years away, so it seemed right for him to revisit his memories. There would be extensive ceremonies at the 9/11 Memorial. Victims' families, the president. Unveiling the waterfalls that now filled the empty foundations of the twin towers. But as the day approached, he grew uneasy about going downtown. The panic he had felt in the weeks after the attacks started creeping back in, a resurgence of old trauma, and I could see he was fighting to keep it at bay.

When we found out the memorial was closed to the general public until after the anniversary, he was relieved. Instead he spotted a listing about a commemorative midday concert at the Metropolitan Museum and said he'd like to go see it. It would be a live performance of *The Disintegration Loops,* a musical composition that had begun as a decayed magnetic tape of an instrumental piece recorded decades before. The composer, William Basinski, came across the tape in his archive in 2001 and was fascinated by the gaps in the sound that occurred where the material of the tape was disintegrating. He selected a segment of the original piece—a mild, moody American pastoral movement—and looped it, digitally manipulating it to alter the effect of the gaps in each loop. He recorded the results as a new, seamless creation that would now be played live by a small orchestra.

When Will was still married to his first wife, he used to experience a kind of preemptive nostalgia. It would arise even before the present had become the past. On Christmas, while he was at home with his family, he would feel a burst of longing for the day he was still at that moment living. He would sit in his Brooklyn apartment and watch his wife and daughter as they opened their gifts, thinking about how much he would miss this day once he was back in the office, once his daughter's school vacation ended. He would envision himself envisioning it all in a week or two. Before it was even a memory, he would see the warm glow of memory shining on them, on him, on the day.

By way of nostalgia, those pretty moments seeped into the gaps left when he blocked out the nearly constant fights he had with his first wife. Nostalgia filled in those gaps with his own benign imaginings, enabling him to not see them. It was a psychic sleight of hand by which his mind revised events as they took place. Nostalgia would distract him, release him, from memories of the ways she had hurt him and the feeling he got when she did. And nostalgia would draw a fine haze over his quiet, soothing drunkenness, over the beers he downed on Christmas Eve to conjure that celebratory glow. And when the holiday ended, nostalgia would buffer him from the fluorescent atmosphere of the midtown offices where he worked as an editor.

It wasn't the past he yearned for. It was the happiness he was not really feeling in the present, and a reality that would enable such happiness. Nostalgia was how he escaped his own life by remaking it, and how he spared himself from knowing escape was what he wanted.

My twelfth year, the third year of my mother's illness, was an in-between time in my family's understanding of our loss, when the initial shock had worn off but we did not yet recognize the change as permanent. For me it was a time of knowing what was happening and yet being unable to consider that it might keep happening indefinitely.

I have only a handful of memories of that year. Moments at my father's house. Moments at school. Moments in the park across the street and at the house of a friend who lived nearby. But the interior of the house my mother rented—she only lived in it that one year—escapes me utterly. I have tried and tried to conjure an image, at least, of my own bedroom, but nothing comes.

I can't know what happened in my missing year, but I suspect it was fairly prosaic: that my mother had a terrible illness and I had to witness it, and witness it, and witness it. Loss to mental illness is a particular thing. For the first few years everything about it read like a dead language turned upside down. My siblings and I couldn't yet see patterns in the strange, imperfect logic of psychosis. Life with my mother was a complicated blend of sense and nonsense. I believe what my gaps hide are innumerable small comments, gestures, and expressions that collectively betrayed this truth.

When the eleventh came, Will was somber. He talked some about 9/11, intertwining the attacks with the impending death of his marriage, which finally came several years later. He spoke of the way the events of the day focused and sharpened his pervasive, amorphous unhappiness, the state of his life and his family at that moment in time—that this was what he most remembered now when he thought of that day. He was quiet as we made our way through the Met to the concert room and found seats. The high-ceilinged room housed the Egyptian sandstone Temple of Dendur, a strange and humbling backdrop. I fell still when the looping music began.

As it progressed, the gaps grew longer. I sank deep into the music's low tones, cadence, hypnotic repetition. With each loop the song felt more like a memory, with suggestions of all we find missing when we retread the past. The loops seemed elastic, pulling at our ears as we listened. They spoke of my own memory more easily stretching as I grew older, encompassing greater spans of years, folding and twisting and pulling ever more distant associations into the orbits of events I have lived.

Something else, too, was taking place: The gaps were coming alive, asserting themselves as insistently as the sounds. I began to feel them as presences. Soon I was picturing them as soft white terry-cloth muffs, or corded mops, or felted dusters, absorbing the sound and eventually pulsating with all they had taken in. They were soft but dense, claiming the space between the notes almost forcefully. After a while an odd perceptual role reversal occurred, and it was the musical notes that felt like interludes. The gaps became the main event. I breathed in time with them, exhaled into the emptiness, felt what I could articulate only in retrospect: that absence is not simple, not simply a void. It is a space packed full.

And there beside that temple, utterly out of context, I may have found the real purpose of my selective amnesia, of Will's nostalgia. Perhaps the true value of both, I felt, lay in their power to simplify. Where Will erased his loss, I made mine entire. We had known that something was lost, but what remained? A shell of a marriage, a foreigner who was my mother. The nostalgia, the gaps—they created completeness where it was not. After all, something always lingers of what is destroyed. And in that long aftermath, faced with all that has not disappeared, we are forced to confront the persistent presence of what remains.

Walking through Central Park that afternoon to get home, I still heard the looping music in my head as we traversed the lawns. We stopped near the northern edge of Onassis Reservoir, where an opening in the bushes gave us a wide view of midtown. Will pointed out the office building where he had worked ten years before. Leaning on the railing, looking over the water at the skyline, he commented on the way, in the months after 9/11, he and his first wife were briefly freed from their battles. It was similar, he said, to the way the whole country seemed for a short while united. He noted that America now seemed almost nostalgic for that awful day.

Ultima Thule

HOW DOES ONE CONCEIVE OF ANOTHER'S HOMELESSNESS? It was a vast unknown, an empty region on the map. Even now, when it is long over, it remains tempting to simply color it in with a pale blue wash, draw in a few low peaks, and tell myself that was all it contained. Maybe label it: Ultima Thule.

There were questions, always, unvoiced. What did Tom notice? How did it feel? The blocky buildings of downtown. The light of low sun. The earthy, salty rot smell coming off the mudflats at low tide. The ravens picking at trash bins, cawing low.

His way of seeing things. Anchorage, always overcast. He once told me he described it to people in Boulder by saying that you could lie down on your back in the park and look up, and the sky would be so high and white above you that you couldn't tell if it was covered by a layer of clouds or if that was just how the light was.

Homelessness as felt by way of psychosis. Some things more acute. Others barely noticed. But which, when, to what degree.

The onset of psychosis is framed by a set of deep changes—radical shifts in how the mind relates to both the world and the self. It goes far beyond losing contact with reality, is more than delusions and hallucinations. It generates not only these bizarre highlights but also the subtler, more pervasive disturbances that make it possible to believe them.

The positive moods that can arise from schizophrenic delusions are distinct in that they tend to seem somehow drained of blood. The ecstasy that Tom sometimes felt was not an infectious cheer, not exuberant glee. It was more akin to a spiritual exultation, a transporting rapture. I am susceptible to others' good moods, easily catching the contagion of laughter, but I could never connect with Tom's psychotic bliss. It was somehow inaccessible, not a joy occurring between people but one reliant on being apart from people.

The delusional mind state of schizophrenia, argues psychologist Louis Sass, is so profoundly different from ordinary states of mind that it involves alterations in experience itself—that is to say, the experience of having experiences. It is a solipsistic mode, paradoxical, in which consciousness itself is transformed, collapsing the distinctions between one's surroundings and oneself. In this state, a person may feel godlike or enslaved, all-controlling or entirely controlled, both at once. He constitutes existence and yet is surveilled by it.

The drizzle, more like fog than rain. Pavement—its contours, its opacity, its gray. The birches' powdery trunks. The alders bent over one another. Water seeping through his clothes. The pall of the sky.

·

After Tom died, I read parts of his journals from the years leading up to the onset of his illness. I couldn't get through them—his near-frantic distress about the way his life was going, how long he had struggled before full-blown psychosis set in. I could feel from the page his aching depression, a stinging kind of loneliness. Nothing he tried seemed to work out, except working out, which he did obsessively. He wanted to study but was failing at school. He wanted to attract girls but couldn't connect with them. And he didn't know why. He felt deeply that something was wrong, but he couldn't figure out what it was. No wonder, then, that when psychosis came in with all its colors it felt like salvation.

There had been a lover, back some time before. We didn't know until long after, when Dad took a wilderness first aid course and she, the instructor, approached him. She had seen the last name on the roster and asked if he was related to Tom. They talked a little while. She said, "He broke my heart." I later found among Tom's journals a note from her with a beautiful drawing of some mountains. Her language was precise, lovely. Why he broke it off, why he never mentioned her—

Among other things, one's perception of time is heavily altered in psychosis. Time loses its continuity, becomes episodic, fragmented, gaping. Much is forgotten, or remembered only as a mood, an atmosphere. Sass noted that people with schizophrenia often speak of "the immobility of time, of the loss of past and future," of difficulty recalling events in the correct order. Events are not processed, integrated, linked to one another in succession, but rather become, as other researchers noted, like "a series of stills." One man with psychosis described it as "the infinite present."

Recently my mother asked me where I went to college. If I had ever lived in Europe. She sounded apologetic, a little embarrassed.

I once met an oral historian who spoke of a "narrative crisis" occurring in people with mental illness, the result of drastic disruptions in the trajectories of their lives and in their recollections of events—a sense of loss of agency, loss of control over not only their lives but also their life stories. Loss of the capacity to shape a life into a story.

By the time Tom was homeless, I had left Alaska for good, chasing down a vague but persistent notion of myself as a writer, following it from Bozeman to graduate school in New Hampshire, then to Santa Fe, where I found work at a magazine (and Will), before moving on to New York and finally Tucson. I only rarely got back to Anchorage, and never for long. In Tom's eight years on the street, I would see him only four times on two visits home—twice for an hour or so and twice for just a few minutes.

One of those times, I spotted him while riding in a friend's car down on our neighborhood's end of Northern Lights Boulevard, the main artery through our part of town, in the residential section that was lined with landscaping of grass and birch trees. We pulled over and I jumped out, but my friend's presence disconcerted him and after only a few exchanges he said he had to go.

·

Experience can be defined, as anthropologist Robert Desjarlais has suggested, as a reflective process of interpretation and
assimilation of our encounters through time. If this is so, does
psychosis create a vacuum of experience? What did Tom make
of our encounters? Did he absorb them, consider them, remember them?

Riding away, I fretted in silence, wondering where he was
walking to. Maybe he would head all the way out past Mom's
old duplex to where a high barbed-wire-topped fence divided
the houses from the boggy woods surrounding the airport.
Maybe he would cut over into Earthquake Park and go out
toward the seaside bluffs on the Coastal Trail, as we all had
long ago, on bikes or Rollerblades or running shoes. Maybe
he would follow the shore and its wide, wild mudflats out
to the overlook at Point Woronzof, where Cook Inlet rolled
into Knik Arm and on a clear day you could see all the way
to Denali.

Where does experience go if it can't proceed forward? For
the homeless mentally ill, Desjarlais proposed, it tends to dissolve into an ongoing succession of shocks and surprises—
distractions interspersed among months or years of an unmoored
kind of stasis.

I have a memory that keeps surfacing. In high school, on overcast nights in winter, the clouds and the snow would trap in
the orange light of the streetlamps, making the sky glow a
dense pinkish orange-brown. Evenings, desperate to get out
of Dad's house, I would sometimes take the Wagoneer and
drive west on Northern Lights near where I would see Tom
walking so many years later—out beyond the airport, past the

runways, to where the city lights ended and the clouds faded to a deep blue-black, turned invisible. I would look up as I drove, watching for the moment I got out from under that toxic sky. Then I would park at a pullout and turn off the car lights and just sit alone in the darkness, listening to the radio.

Was he beset? Was he thrown wide? Was psychosis a land of many promises? Did he know he was a prisoner there?

A Tree Falling

TOM'S SLIDE INTO HOMELESSNESS OCCURRED IN SMALL,
successive stages. In a way, I was never sure quite how it happened, though some of it is clear enough in retrospect. He
had no job and did not get one. He ran out of money and was
churning through our mother's savings until Adrienne rescued
the last of it by getting his name removed from the account.
He had to sell his car, and eventually that money ran out too.
In other words, he was a functioning adult until he was not.
But we never knew exactly when or how he lost his apartment,
when or how he came to crash on friends' couches, when or
how he began having run-ins with the cops. Nor did we mark
the beginning of his habit of walking incessantly, roaming the
streets and bike paths of west Anchorage as he would for the
rest of his life. It was only much later that we learned he had
been spending whole days driving around town, marking up
a city map with notes and arrows, pursuing a delusion about
women he believed had been kidnapped. Tom was a tree falling in the forest, and for a long time none of us were sure he
had made a sound.

His first arrest, in 2004, was for trespassing. He had been loitering at Ben Boeke, an ice arena near downtown, and when the management asked him to leave, he refused. He told none of us, however, so no one posted bail and he was sent to a minimum-security facility, Cordova Center, to await charges. Within days, he stepped outside to take out the trash and bolted. But a few weeks later he was arrested again. So followed a criminal charge: escape. The authorities by then understood that Tom was dealing with mental illness, and he was given the option of proceeding through the state's Coordinated Resources Project (CRP) court, a mental-health-based alternative to the standard criminal court. But he declined the option and so spent a month in jail.

Finally things got worse enough that it seemed they might start to get better. That December he somehow made his way fifty miles north to Wasilla, where, at a Blockbuster video store, he began to feel that he was "about to hear the sound of a woman scream." I know this because he later described it to a doctor at Alaska Psychiatric Institute, the state-run hospital in Anchorage. It seems he was embroiled in his delusion, trying to rescue someone, sensing and following her almost-sounds. I know, too, that the sensation was upsetting—so much so that he changed it, in his mind, to the cry of an eagle. Then he started running, heading back toward Anchorage. Thirty miles south he found himself in Eagle River, cold and confused and unsure of how he had gotten there. He went into a Carrs grocery store to warm up and, afraid he would get kicked out, decided to pretend he worked there. The police picked him up after customers complained that he was following them around the store and talking to himself. He was perceived, the API report states, as "agitated and threatening."

He was taken first to Providence Hospital's psychiatric ER,

where they ran some tests and stabilized him on olanzapine, an antipsychotic and sedative. When tests for alcohol and street drugs came up negative, he was transferred to API. There he told the psychiatrist he controlled a TV channel that was being broadcast into space, that he needed neither sleep nor food due to internal energy that kept building itself up, that he spent his waking hours creating businesses in his mind, and that he was hearing voices. "The patient," the doctor wrote, "indicates his break was very sudden, one day thinking clearly, and the next in a 'dream.'"

Tom surely knew, then, that his brain wasn't functioning right. This must have been why he cooperated with the treatment offered during his thirty-day stay at API. It is unnerving now to consider how long ago he first grasped the kind of trouble he was in, and even more so to imagine his reaction to the news of his diagnosis: "schizophrenia, undifferentiated type." How it must have surprised him, felt like a blow. The power of the name of the thing.

With Tom's new trespassing charge still pending, Dad convinced him to allow the case to proceed through the CRP court. At Tom's sentencing, the state mandated that he complete one year of outpatient treatment for his schizophrenia in lieu of punishment—twice-weekly group therapy, regular meetings with a psychiatrist, and a daily dose of risperidone, a common antipsychotic medication. Tom went to live with Dad, and for the next year and a half, Dad assiduously took care of him, cooking his meals, making sure he got to his appointments, renting movies for them to watch together, and each morning handing him his antipsychotic pill. But Tom wasn't convinced that he had schizophrenia. And although he had chosen this path, he seemed surprised by the medication mandate and felt that he had been forced, or tricked, into treatment. The idea made him flatly furious, so much so that he wrote letters to George W. Bush and Dick Cheney expressing his outrage and asking for release.

The word *anosognosia* began to pepper our conversations—the medical term for lack of insight. Impairment or absence of insight affects about half of people with schizophrenia, rendering sufferers unaware that they are ill. Research suggests that this occurs because the illness damages specific structures and networks in the brain that are responsible for such recognition. We weren't sure how much anosognosia was to blame for Tom's resistance and how much to attribute to denial or simple anger at being forced into something, but I hoped it was mostly the latter, because I wasn't sure there was anything we could do if it was the former.

There were reasons to think Tom would ultimately agree to stay on the risperidone. He had never been a troublemaker, was not a combative or contrarian type. He had a solid and gentle personality, and I had rarely seen him be impulsive or aggressive or extreme. On the contrary, in our family he had usually played the part of the peacekeeper. But he could also be stubborn, and I knew he must be terrified of schizophrenia, as we all were, and that he surely felt humiliated about what had happened. I worried, too, about the distinct mental rigidity I had often seen in Mom—what the twentieth-century psychiatrist Karl Jaspers described as a "specific schizophrenic incorrigibility." It is a hard quality to convey in words. In my experience, most people can't believe a human is capable of such intransigence for no apparent reason until they see it for themselves.

Dad soon discovered that although Tom took his risperidone each morning when prompted, he often cheeked his pills—pretended to swallow them while stashing them in the side of his mouth—and then spat them out and hid them in the potted plants or the folds of his knit cap. Dad would find them when he cleaned. But he couldn't get Tom to stop. All he could do was keep pressing him to take the pills and to bring up any concerns with the psychiatrist, hoping that staying on the medication would eventually clear Tom's mind enough that he could recognize its necessity.

If you Google "how to convince someone with schizophrenia to get treatment," you soon discover a vast network of distraught families grappling for answers. The first suggestions you'll find, from places like the National Institutes of Health and WebMD, usually involve trying to break through resistance by being supportive and allaying fears. Experts counsel family members to avoid sounding threatening, focus on concern for the sufferer's safety, and keep the discussion among people he trusts and feels close to. It requires partnering with the sufferer as well as influencing him without being controlling or intolerant. What isn't said is that there is instinct and talent and skill involved in being convincing under these circumstances, and not everyone is good at it.

I was not good at it. When I called Tom at Dad's house, a little stunned to be so suddenly in contact with him after many long months, I didn't bring up his circumstances at all. I didn't know why exactly. It was that same feeling of impossibility I had always had, and maybe, too, I was afraid to say the wrong thing. This was only made worse when Dad told me that Tom had said to him, "Don't tell my sisters I've been in jail." I knew things I wasn't supposed to know, and I couldn't find a way to reach beyond that.

I couldn't even talk to myself about it, really. Something inside me just stopped—stopped me up. After our calls, I would try to record our conversations in my journal, but every time, I found myself going softly blank, losing the thread. As soon as I touched the keyboard I would feel the air growing thick, resisting my movements. My mind would go still and I would sit as if hypnotized, fingers useless on the keys. Eventually I would give up, stand, walk out into the kitchen and make a salad or open a beer. The words, locked up, lay there until they slipped away, soon forgotten. In one journal entry, after trying and failing, I wrote simply, "Schizophrenia takes even my words away from me."

In the meantime, Tom at least mellowed out. Slowly he began to seem more like himself. He and Dad got along well enough, and Dad talked often to him about making a commitment to getting better over the long term. As Tom reconnected with reality and began to acknowledge he had been delusional, Dad found ways to help him engage with life again. Tom got a job as a cashier and stocker at the giant REI store not far from Dad's house, where his friend Zach noticed how well he could multitask, chatting with customers and counting money and answering phones all at once—such a change from the distracted, disoriented person he had been. But in other ways, he was far from his old self. At one point, Dad left town for a couple of weeks with Tom as house sitter and returned to find the plants dying and the kitchen strewn with empty beer bottles and cereal bowls. Another time, Dad came home from running errands to discover that Tom had left a burner flaming on the stove.

When I visited home that summer, things seemed okay in a tentative, bland kind of way. Tom's hallucinations and delusions had faded markedly and his wit had returned. He joked sometimes, smiled a little, sat with us like he wanted to be part of what was going on. But he was stiff and laconic, his face nearly empty of emotion, and he held his body very square—facing forward from the couch, hands resting lightly on knees—no matter how the rest of us were lounging and sprawling. His whole way of being felt repetitive, simplified, restricted somehow—a quality captured surprisingly well in the psychiatric terms I discovered that describe it: *stereotyped gestures, flattened affect, impoverished speech.* These were among the illness's negative and cognitive symptoms—deficits, impairments. And in Tom, they were legion.

Perhaps this was why, though antipsychotics were a key starting point, it would take more than pills to heal a brain such as Tom's. Schizophrenia disrupts many brain functions, from movement to motivation to memory, and often the most debilitating symptoms never fully resolve. In Tom's case, the risperidone appeared to have only moderately helped with his negative symptoms, even after six months. But we had no way of knowing what dosage he was actually getting—how often he managed to spit out his pills. For a while I thought Tom must have disliked how the risperidone made him feel, but Tom told Dad he felt no side effects, aside from a new sensitivity to cold that led him to sleep under extra blankets. So I couldn't guess why he resisted the pills. Perhaps, I thought, he simply could not believe that the doubt and boredom that accompanied sanity could be what it meant to get well.

I was conflicted about the mandated treatment. Its existence gave us a chance to help, but the power to compel Tom to take medication was a cold and ambivalent comfort. He had been stripped of so much and now could not even claim the dignity of being in control of the chemicals that shaped his mind. It seemed clear enough that this contributed to his resistance. And yet I could not have taken seriously the idea that he could manage at that time without his medication, especially when I considered how the illness itself was clouding his judgment. All I wanted was for the symptoms to stop.

I would later learn of research that supported this intuition, suggesting that schizophrenic processes actively damage the brain in ways that may be irreversible. Doctors encourage early intervention because preventing or shortening psychosis has been shown to increase a sufferer's chances of recovery over time. The less time a person spends in a psychotic state, the better his overall functioning is likely to be in the long run and the more likely it is that medication can help him. And we had already spent two years accomplishing nothing.

The work that fell to me was that of listening. We knew Tom would likely never confide in Dad the way he might with Adrienne or me, especially with the stakes as they were. But I was still too hesitant to get anywhere. While we were in town that summer, staying with Tom so Dad could visit his mother in Colorado, I danced around the subject awkwardly, talking only about shallow things, approaching the issue obtusely, trying to somehow secretly glimpse Tom's thoughts without saying *medication* or *mental illness* out loud. It felt like the topic of schizophrenia was just under the surface all the time, pressing up at us both. One day as Tom showed Adrienne and me around REI, he mentioned some idea and I laughingly commented that it sounded crazy. He froze midsentence and then turned to look at a rack of shirts. Adrienne glared at me—accusatory, horrified. I looked back at her sheepishly, as stunned as she was. It was as if the word's newly taboo quality had forced it from my mouth.

In retrospect, I suspect that Tom wanted to talk to us about his mental health. Or at least wanted it to be easy to talk about. When I think about it now, I just think that we were all so young. I was still new to the concept of recovery from schizophrenia—the idea that, although there is no cure, its sufferers can nonetheless live meaningful and productive lives, often managing their symptoms well enough to get degrees, build careers, find partners. I didn't yet understand that overcoming the illness wasn't about shutting it down so much as finding a path through it. None of us really thought that way back then. It didn't occur to me that non-medication therapies like counseling, skill building, and social involvement might all be integral to Tom's recovery. And anyway, his mandated treatment plan didn't offer that kind of help, aside from group sessions with addicts and others he had little in common with.

Tom's feelings did sometimes come through, however, almost too clearly. When I asked him how he liked working at REI, he said flatly, "It's really boring." And he looked at me straight, holding my gaze for a moment to mark his point. I came away feeling a little shaken. I understood that he did not like his life.

When it came to Tom's plans, it was hard to tell if he was just saying what he knew everyone wanted to hear. That fall, Dad got him enrolled in a writing class at UAA, and he obviously enjoyed it. And when winter came on, he and Dad started taking trips up to Girdwood to ski together at Mount Alyeska. Growing up, we had spent countless weekends on that mountain, first with our mother, who taught us to ski after she bought her condo, and then just as often with Dad, who had skied as a boy in Colorado and showed us how to tackle the harder terrain, driving us the hour each way on day trips until he bought a cabin within walking distance of the lifts. Tom, a near-expert skier, clearly loved bombing down the mountain the way he used to. But he still showed little motivation in life outside of the activities Dad coordinated for him. And he insisted that his delusional state wouldn't happen again. He believed his psychosis was a one-time problem, not a sign of a chronic condition.

Whenever you meet resistance in your efforts to convince a person with schizophrenia to accept care, experts advise, try to work around rigid beliefs rather than attempting to dismantle them. Don't argue with delusions, they counsel, and don't focus on points of contention. Find common ground, any common ground. Listen respectfully and empathize. One book advocated circumventing the question of diagnosis altogether, focusing instead on goals you can both agree on, such as addressing specific symptoms like tormenting voices or difficulty sleeping. This "motivational interviewing" approach, when I learned of it, struck me as brilliant. But in our lives, applying new skills was rarely simple. We tried them haphazardly, sporadically, never fully grasping how they could lead to the breakthrough we desired, never fully able to step outside our own fears and prejudices.

Other times, Tom's situation was out of our control. At one point, Dad took Tom to meet with a woman about applying for subsidized housing, a benefit for which his illness made him eligible. Beforehand, Dad called the woman and explained the need to tread lightly on the topic of Tom's diagnosis, as he was sensitive about his mental health and would resist being labeled a schizophrenic. She agreed to be careful, but then during the meeting, as she began explaining the process to Tom, she announced, "As soon as we have your psych eval we can put this paperwork through." On hearing "psych eval"—

psychiatric evaluation—Tom got up and walked out. Dad, beside himself, turned to the woman as he stood to go and said, "That was it. We won't get another chance."

In February, Tom graduated from his treatment program. Despite the pitfalls, Dad felt confident about his progress. "He has learned so much in this past year," he wrote me in an email. But with the state no longer requiring Tom to take medication, he soon said that he wanted to quit the risperidone. His psychiatrist urged him to rethink his decision, but he was sure. They made a plan to slowly taper off the pills over the next five months. Dad was hopeful that if Tom started having psychotic symptoms again he would raise his dose back up, but as spring became summer, he watched Tom slip contentedly back into psychosis.

When convincing fails, greater pressure is sometimes recommended. In families, this usually takes the form of firmly establishing conditions and putting forth hard choices between treatment and negative consequences. It is, in the language of addiction, about not being an enabler while also not being overly punitive. When the state does this, it's called "benevolent coercion"—and Tom had already received some in the form of the CRP court's treatment mandate. So far it hadn't worked. Now, as what had been built began again to fall away, Dad applied more of his own pressure, more intensely.

And as he did so, their relationship suffered. Off his medication, Tom became slovenly and forgetful, triggering Dad's anger and stoking arguments about his future. It was hard to tell how clearly he understood what Dad was trying to do, but any partnership that they had built was collapsing. In July, Tom went off the risperidone altogether. Around that time, he was fired from his job at REI. Their fighting grew worse, culminating one day in August when Tom raged in the doorway, so amped and angry that Dad took pause, stood back, realized he had no idea what was going to happen next. Tom left and did not return.

Where he went, where he slept, I don't know. But a few days later, when Dad wasn't home, he broke into the house by jimmying the lock with a credit card and grabbed an old checkbook from his bedroom. It was for the account he had once shared with our mother, but the account had been closed for over a year and he didn't seem to realize there was no money left in it. He checked in to a quaint little inn downtown and started making purchases. Collectors' coins, geodes, a framed painting, a silk Persian rug, heart-shaped pendants for some secret or imagined love. The police got involved when an officer spotted Tom loitering and, noticing he was holding several antique silver dollars, started asking questions. Tom said he hoped to sell the items later at a higher price and that he wanted someday to be an art dealer. He ended up showing the officer the checkbook he had used. Within days he was charged with one count of theft and three counts of issuing a bad check. Two of these were felony charges.

The owner of the rug store, it turned out, knew Tom by name and said he had stopped in often to examine the rug, once sitting and staring at it for two solid hours. When Tom checked out of the hotel a week later, he left the rug behind with a note to the general manager, saying that it was a thank-you gift for his stay there. It was worth $2,600.

Dad learned of the arrest when an officer called to question him. As the investigation proceeded, he talked to the attorneys and officers involved, explaining each time that he was sure Tom had not intentionally committed a crime. Tom was deemed eligible for the CRP court again, and ultimately the

DA dropped both felony charges. But this time, Tom declined the CRP option. He was done with mandated treatment. In September, he pled no contest to the misdemeanors and spent another month in jail.

A look at the message boards on Schizophrenia.com, a website offering information and community for anyone affected by the illness, shows how many others have debated the merits and dangers of coercion, particularly its harshest tactics. One father explains that he is considering telling his son he must move out, though he knows this will lead to homelessness, and a mother counsels him not to do it unless he can stand firm until some good comes of it. Another mother states that she refuses to let her son live with her as long as he resists taking medication, but emphasizes that this doesn't mean she's abandoning him, that she still gives him money and shows him respect and affection. A man with schizophrenia expresses gratitude that his own parents never kicked him out when he refused treatment, saying he would not have gotten better without their unwavering support. Another states that if he hadn't been kicked out he would never have sought help—he had to come to it on his own.

It seems that nothing works for everybody and everything works for somebody—even this harshest alternative, designed as it is to make a person so uncomfortable in his illness that he is pushed to choose treatment. What is most likely to work, what works most often—this I do not know, though related research suggests that the gentler, subtler forms of coercion are more effective, as they enable the sufferer to retain a sense of agency. Perhaps something would have been different, then, if Tom had received individual talk therapy, or if any of us had known how to help him work through his fears. I would learn much later that, in a moment of coherence and vulnerability, he had told his friend Zach outright that he stopped taking the risperidone because he felt "embarrassed." Embarrassed by his circumstances, by his diagnosis, by the state of his life. It must have just seemed easier not to face it, easier to be psychotic.

Dad, believing that he needed to step up the pressure, considered his next move. I know he thought long and hard about it, carefully weighed the risks of Tom's living on the street versus continuing on with untreated schizophrenia. I dreaded the idea of Tom being homeless—could not even fathom it, really. But Dad would make the decision on his own and I knew I could not change his mind. And truly, I wasn't sure that I should. Perhaps it was a hopeless kind of optimism, but I thought maybe it was worth it to let him hit bottom. Maybe, in the words of one family friend, we just needed to wait until Tom got "sick and tired of being sick and tired."

Dad tried to visit Tom while he was in jail, but Tom refused to see him. So Dad wrote him a letter that he later delivered. It read: "I want you to try and remember how much I love you and care for you." It read: "It is obvious now that you have a problem that you are refusing to accept" and "By allowing you to live here, I am enabling you to avoid making the decisions that you must make." It read: "My heart aches to help you."

Dad explained that he did not intend to let Tom into the house again, but said he hoped he would stay in touch and that he would like to take him to dinner from time to time. He closed the letter with a mention of another young man he had recently met, who had problems similar to Tom's but was now in recovery and no longer needed to take medication, adding, "It is possible for some, and perhaps for you." He provided the man's name and phone number and encouraged Tom to get in touch with him.

So Dad made his impossible bargain. He changed the locks and alarm codes to the house. On Tom's release date, he took him a backpack containing some of his things, including his last paychecks from REI. And Tom became homeless just as winter was setting in.

Mr. Rain Jacket

AS TOM'S EXPERIENCE TRANSFORMED, SO DID MY EXPERI-
ence of his experience. I found myself unable to discern a
story line in what was happening, to connect the sudden shifts
and discoveries that periodically shook me. Tom's homelessness was to me, perhaps as it was for him, just as Desjarlais
suggested—a succession of random surprises that burst like
fireworks through long periods of seeming emptiness. Here
was my own narrative crisis, my own bewilderment.

How Tom survived so long out on the street eludes me still.
Much of it, I'm sure, had to do with his own strengths. Since
adolescence he had been deeply concerned with how to live,
how to do right by others, how to be. He was quick to defend
the weak, to tell you to stop being a jerk, to point out how
you were being unfair. In illness, this solidified into a rigid
and high-minded moral code to which he adhered strictly, and
which seemed to be part of how he avoided encounters with
people who could do him real harm.

It was not that he blended in. Aside from his odd demeanor,

And beneath that, pushed down: If Tom were to do something—something that had once been the kind of thing he would never do. If one day I might learn that Tom had harmed someone, intentionally or not. I felt that the world was asking me something, something serious and necessary, and I had no idea how to answer.

This was where, for a while, the story became entirely about fear.

This was where the story looped back, many years, to a boy I had known in high school. Terrance, a grade above me, a champion wrestler, loved by the wrestling team, close with my friends Sean and Kevin. He was albino, African American, tall and gregarious, and it was rumored that he had been held back in fifth grade. You would see him in the halls, joking around, grinning in the sunglasses he wore indoors to protect his fragile pink eyes. I had met him one day when he meandered up to my locker and playfully told me he was taking a poll, and would I be willing to participate? He was trying to identify what percentage of girls were bitches, he explained, and to determine if I was a bitch, he had one question: Could he have my phone number? I stared at him, more fascinated than appalled—took in the varsity jacket, the acne, the surprising white of his eyelashes when he pulled off his shades. He was sort of bobbing, graceful, all fluid energy. No, I said, and never talked to him again.

It would be another decade before Sean told me more about Terrance. Told me he was intelligent, sensitive, far more so than people gave him credit for. Told me that he, like Sean, had bipolar disorder so severe that he sometimes had psychotic episodes. That some doctors even believed Terrance had schizophrenia. Sean's episodes, by then, were in the past, his illness under control. We were looking back on what had happened when we were seniors, when Terrance was a year out of high school.

There is no real way to introduce it. Terrance took his ten-year-old brother hostage at gunpoint on an overpass above an Anchorage boulevard. He had a revolver cocked and pointed at the child. He was in a standoff with the police, ranting about Martians to a negotiator while snipers trained their rifles on him. A woman in a nearby home, watching the scene unfold, grabbed her camcorder and started filming. Terrance did not surrender.

When the police went to Terrance's home, they found his mother and eight-year-old sister dead in the bathroom.

This was where the story became incoherent.

And the woman with the camcorder—she called the evening news shows and sold them copies of her tape. *A Current Affair* aired it as well. And I, at eighteen, saw the fuzzy black-and-white glow of cheap footage on high zoom—a white head beside a smaller, darker head. I heard the sharp snap of the gunshot. I saw the pale blob that was Terrance jerk quickly and slump, falling softly sideways. And the woman said, "Oh my God they just blew his head off."

I tell you all of this because it taught me some things. For weeks, my high school was in a furor over why Terrance had killed his family members. The papers reported that he came from poverty, that a genetic condition was slowly blinding him, that he had struggled with domestic problems. That his wrestling coaches had believed he had overcome those challenges. That he had recently been hospitalized for mental health reasons. That he had said, on the overpass, that his little brother was "an alien from another planet." One reporter wrote, "You can never see to the bottom of a man's soul."

To me it didn't seem to have much to do with Terrance's soul. Psychosis—my mother's, at least—was as familiar to me as the bed I slept in. When I heard the bit about the alien, I guessed that Terrance had had a psychotic break. That he hadn't grasped that he was killing his own kin, or even humans, for that matter. What made less sense to me was the part about how it was that I watched him die.

Many years later, I would learn of research showing that delusions are shaped in part by local culture, and that Americans with psychosis are more likely to have violence-themed hallucinations. I would learn, too, that Terrance himself had been shaped by violence. That he had once been shot in a drive-by, and that the handgun he carried that day was believed to belong to his older brother. But I knew none of this at the time. I knew only that Terrance's death seeped into me, stayed with me, became like an unshakable fact—an object lesson. That the lesson was indecipherable only made it more powerful.

In September, Tom was arrested again. This time, a young woman called the police saying that a man had walked into her house, stood in the living room as she told him to leave, and then lingered outside, peering into the windows. He was picked up and charged with disorderly conduct. Specifically: peeping. "How is that even the actual name of it?" I demanded to Adrienne when I later read the official report. She grimaced, shaking off the willies.

What was the right side of things? How do you know a person? What I mean is that something had to come undone, had to be torn away, to make room for the possibility of violence or predation in Tom. And I didn't know exactly what that something was or whether it had been lost or if it could be taken from him at all.

Did it matter that randomly, at a soccer practice, Sean's friend Matt happened to hear the young woman who had called the police talking about what had happened? She spoke of a frightening incident with a stranger who stepped into her house early one morning while she was still in her nightclothes. She said that ever since that day she had been lying awake at night, had been afraid to be home alone. But Matt recognized her description of the man—that yellow raincoat—and asked his name. And he said, "Oh, no, no! It's not like that!" He explained that he knew Tom, describing what he could of his illness—his delusions, his belief that young women were being kidnapped, his determination to rescue them, his desire not to hurt but to help.

I was glad that Matt could speak with confidence about Tom's good intentions. His assessment must have been influenced by Sean, who knew Tom's illness as intimately as anyone. But it was still disconcerting that the delusion centered so strongly on young women, however altruistically. And I felt like a cliché—the sister avowing that her brother was not capable of harming another person. I would think of that young woman, off and on, for a long time. I would think about how, some time later, she spoke to Matt again and told him that since the time of their conversation, her panic had vanished, faded away. I would think of her and I would feel relief and nausea, all at once.

I was bolstered when I read the other letters written in response to the "Mr. Rain Jacket" column, the ones that were printed. The deputy chief of police wrote that the columnist could have helped Tom by calling the Anchorage Police Department and asking for a "welfare check." He explained that an officer with Crisis Intervention Team training—one skilled at de-escalating tensions and offering support to mentally unstable or ill individuals—would have assessed the situation and intervened if necessary. The chairwoman of the Alaska Mental Health Board defended Tom with research indicating that stress, substance abuse, and certain personality traits were much stronger contributors to violence than mental illness, and that only less severe mental health problems were significantly associated with violent acts. She wrote of studies showing that the severely mentally ill were no more likely to be violent than the rest of us. The medical director of Anchorage Community Mental Health Services wrote that "the vast majority" of people with mental illness were "neither violent nor dangerous," and that they were far more likely to be victims of violence than perpetrators. This was the part that unnerved me. Seven times more likely, I read from another source around that time.

I can only infer how these events affected Tom, but it seems that something shifted that summer, something that would never really be undone. After Tom was ordered not to go within five hundred feet of the young woman's house—and this, I imagine, would have been explained to him in no uncertain terms—he established a rule for himself that he would no longer touch women. Three years later, I would ask him if I could have a hug and he would say, "No. No hugging." A year after that he would say the same to Adrienne, and when she asked why, she would see he was still confused about what exactly had gone wrong with the young woman, still feeling it was safer to stick to his rule than to risk another incident.

Over time it became apparent, as well, that he responded in equally categorical terms to Dad's letter barring him from the house. Soon Dad would be inviting Tom over and encouraging him to stay longer, and Tom would be the one to turn away, to decide it was time to leave, as if some great commandment had proclaimed that he could never again spend a night at his former home. What drove his thinking seemed a blend of schizophrenic rigidity and a burgeoning paranoia, a symptom that was slowly becoming central to his experience of the illness.

At the time, though, none of this registered with us. We didn't have enough information, couldn't see it yet. Nor could we know what happened while Tom was in jail for that peeping charge. Going through his court records after he died, I found something—something that didn't seem to fit anywhere until it felt like the crux of all that followed. While Tom was being held in custody and awaiting a hearing, things got bad for him somehow. What exactly took place, I don't know. I would not have known anything happened at all were it not for a brief note on one otherwise uninteresting page. Most of them were complicated forms with a few boxes checked here and there, indicating, for instance, that on September 26, 2007, bail was set at $250 and the defendant was not present. But on one form, in a lined portion reserved for notes, there were two words, unexplained: SUICIDE WATCH.

When I later went seeking an explanation for this, I found a statement in the *Anchorage Daily News* about a psychiatrist who had practiced at both API and the Department of Corrections: "Sperbeck . . . has seen that inmates suffering from severe mental illness will often be targeted by predators within the prison population who try to extort privileges, services and property from them." Tom might, therefore, have been driven to harm himself. Or, as Sperbeck explained, such inmates were sometimes put in isolation at their own request, as a means of protection—though in the long run, this was "very harmful to them."

After that, Tom did not get arrested again for a long time. He had clearly decided that jail was not where he wanted to be, and he must have gotten better at avoiding trouble. That left him on his own, alone on the street.

Dades Gorge

YOU SEE IT SOMETIMES IN CAR COMMERCIALS. SPECTACULAR, plunging. The steep desert ridge, the hairpin road, the sharp edge.

Adrienne and I were tired by then, two weeks on in Morocco, accustomed to avoiding eye contact in the streets as we traveled, although the men—Berbers (Moors, I at some point realized)—were the most beautiful we had seen anywhere. Strange, to be fending them off when we wanted to stare. But in Boumalne Dades we had been spooked immediately. On a walk, on a small path, two had followed us at a distance.

The town was clustered at the base of the rocks. The color of sand. There were no other tourists at the hotel. But Adrienne was sick and collapsed in the bathroom, hit her head on the thick wooden door. Across the street I bought antibiotics. She slept and we waited two winter days.

In the café several men gathered. There was propane there, a heater lit just for us, the paying customers. They told us this, turning toward us with open faces, welcoming, curious. They hovered, served us tea and soup.

A young man glared, then addressed us in Berber. I threw out a few words, all I knew. *"Azul!"* (Hello.) *"Mush!"* (Cat.) He stared, and then switched to English and showed me how to write my name in his ancient, alien alphabet. Others spoke of the Arabs, their long-ago conquerors, bringers of Islam.

A bus driver came and went. Soft face, soft voice. He told us the Berber women had too many babies, one every year, no medicine. He looked at us with gentle eyes and said, "The women here suffer more than the men."

We had met one young woman at the *hammam,* tried to speak to her as we paid for our baths, found no common language but our tattoos—hers on her face, ours on our backs. With gestures we asked how hers was done, and she held up a safety pin.

Hassan, the young man, had been briefly to university. He would not get married. He did not want his grandma with her ear to the door on his wedding night. Did not want the bloody sheet hung like a flag out the window. There was rage in his voice. But he wrote in my journal, "You are mazing."

In the fields, grandmothers bent under loads of sticks, hauling them home for cooking fires. Black fabric cloaked them, covering all but a single eye.

Something in Hassan was familiar—his look, intense and unreadable. "Like Tom," I said to Adrienne, at first hesitant to point it out. I had a feeling that nothing could make it better for him. Found myself hoping I was wrong.

Why did they tell us all this? And what could we do with it, except remember? The bus driver said he had tried to hand out birth control pills, but the women would not take them. He had even tried to trick them by saying it was candy. We looked at each other. "The women here," he said, "suffer too much."

That is what they told us. They, with their history, their poverty, their dry cold wind. Their Berber letter *yaz,* signifying freedom, its shape like a man with his arms up. Themselves, men. The rocks of Dades outside, stacked and shorn. The world, cleft. And we, their pale confessors.

Theory of Mind

A TERM SCIENTISTS USE TO REFER TO THE HUMAN CAPACITY
to imagine oneself into the mind of another—to infer another's
mental states, gleaning thoughts, feelings, and intentions solely
through context and actions and gestures. Theory of mind is
commonly impaired in those who suffer from mental illnesses
such as schizophrenia. This seems to suggest that most of us
can fairly easily imagine ourselves into others' experiences,
even those of the mentally ill.

This matters to me because when I talk about mental illness
I am talking about my mother, about my brother. Terms like
schizoaffective and *schizophrenia* and *psychosis* bring me into
the cosmos of their delusions.

"That cat used to stand outside my door at night and talk
to me," my mother told me. She imitated the voice of the
cat—a melodious sort of meowling that at times resembled the
sounds of words. "It was prophetic," she went on. "One time
it said, 'Don't go outside tomorrow.' So I stayed in."

I can't tell you what she saw, or heard, or felt, that led
her to make these statements. When we with less spectacu-

lar minds, the so-called neurotypical, attempt to imagine the inner reality of someone like my mother, or anyone whose mind functions in ways dramatically different from our own, we usually fall drastically short. We assume similarity until proven otherwise. And when faced with evidence of difference, we struggle to incorporate it. We often refuse to accept it, clinging to the belief that other minds work more or less like our own.

Impairments in theory of mind, it seems, go both ways.

.   .   .

The work of understanding sometimes requires finding another way in, a back door.

I'll tell you: I had a dream, a startling dream. It happened while Will was out of town, gone from our house in Tucson for a few days to take his daughter to college. While he was away, the exterminator came, and I was glad. The previous week, plopping down on the sofa and pulling a small throw blanket over my body, I had discovered a slightly crushed, not entirely dead scorpion. I had lain frozen for a second before gingerly carrying the blanket outside, where I quickly snapped it to toss the scorpion over our yard's back wall. When Will finds scorpions, on the other hand, he speaks to them and carefully scoops them into cups for release outside. A Scorpio himself, he fancies them to be his kin.

Family. Scorpions. Home. My dream fused all of it. The results were awesome and terrible.

I was in a large old building not unlike the mansion my grandparents once owned, a hacienda-style ranch house amid vast lawns. Windows were open, their long white curtains waving. Through those rooms I wandered until, looking down, I saw an enormous scorpion a foot or so before me. I stepped back; it hopped forward. I backed up again, but it pursued me. For a few moments I did a little dance to avoid it, until finally it stood still.

It was much larger than a real scorpion. It even seemed to expand slightly as I examined it. And it was not black or beige, but blue—a soft, cloudy, chalky blue tinged here and there with green and gray and purple. Its back, too, was unusual, consisting of several large chitinous scales like those on the tail of a lobster. Along the sides of its body ran its many legs. Then it unfurled and stood upright, revealing a scaled belly and a head that was not arachnoid at all—more human than arthropod, yet hard, helmeted. It jumped at me again.

Schizophrenic delusions share some features in common with a healthy brain's nighttime dreams. Research suggests that both arise by way of the same processes—those of the brain's default-mode network, which is active when the mind is released from the constraints of focusing on specific tasks. Default network activity enables distant regions of the brain to communicate and discern relationships among disparate ideas.

Perhaps this is why, like dreams, schizophrenic delusions seem to be filtered through the emotional preoccupations that color human days. I have read that the extraordinary dangers that can appear in such delusions often originate in smaller, more personal fears. My mother once believed that a comet was about to destroy the earth; she was at the time going through a divorce.

Some researchers hypothesize that random images, mismatched with strong emotions, feed the paranoia that has gripped people like my mother and brother. Perhaps this link-age is how the betrayals of schizophrenia begin. Perhaps it is how all betrayals begin.

"Don't go on any boats for a while," my mother said. "You might go through the locks to another colony. You could end up on the wrong planet." What locks, what colony, what planet. I no longer ask. "Thousands of crabs were swept through the locks recently," she exclaimed. "A whole migration!"

. . .

In my dream, terrified, I searched for some barrier to put between the scorpion and me. I ran, but it pursued me from room to room until we came to an open outer door and it hopped outside. I slammed the door shut behind it. But the door was old weathered wood with no seal at the threshold, and the scorpion came—impossibly, given its size—right through a crack. I bolted to another room and tried the same thing with another outside door, but again, after jumping out, the scorpion slipped back in. Finally I found a door with a solid seal and shut it out for good, thinking: *It won't survive in the cold.* Then suddenly the air outside was frigid, as if I had made it so. I looked through the door's glass window and watched.

The scorpion stood fully upright, shocked by the icy air, and froze into something perfectly crystalline and still. Its head bore even more of a face now and it was nearly a foot tall. Its blue skeleton turned clear as glass while its body widened and flattened, so that all its inner organs were on display. Now it was almost a little man shaped like a spade, reminding me of those glass figurines you find in trinket shops. It was masterfully sculpted. Each glass organ hung suspended in its own glass cage and was colored through, bright and translucent. I noticed the heart, its reds and violets and blues.

When I awoke, my heart raced. I pulsed with the panic of a prey animal. Then, as the fear eased, I lay in astonishment. That I could have invented this. That I still saw the details as clearly as in life.

Later I wondered: What if I saw my scorpion while awake? In this room, at my feet. As if it were real, really there before me. *Don't go outside tomorrow. Don't go on any boats.* The thought nearly choked me, nearly wrung me to tears.

and obsidian skies folding down over him, the bright sharp darkness of nineteen-hour nights. The air crisp as if shot through with ice. It made your eyes water and then froze the tears against your lashes. And then there was the thick, dull feeling of body parts slowly going numb. That wooden sensation all around your thighs, and your earlobes and toes too, if you weren't careful.

I dreamed of being the one to hand Tom a wool cap, a thick coat, some flannel-lined carpenter pants. Sturdy leather hiking boots, weatherproofed, solid—or fat Sorels, rubber-and-leather snow boots lined with sheepskin.

During cold snaps, Dad would drive around looking for him, stopping if he saw him on the sidewalk, inviting him back to the house for dinner and a shower. Tom often said yes, just for a while. Sometimes Dad would give him a haircut, do his laundry. Always he gave him some cash. And then Tom would want to leave again, go back outside.

In the background, memories. Dark evenings when, home from college, I'd been in the habit of putting on long johns under my jeans and a down coat and a fleece hat and going out walking. Alone in the streets of Turnagain neighborhood, between the intermittent streetlights, trudging through the layer of scraped, compressed snow. As I roamed past the houses we had always lived among, hugging the edges of the plowed roads, I communed with the split-level homes—their wooden siding, their mailboxes and garage doors and driveways. I was looking for ghosts, I think, and trying to unravel the secret of what my life was.

.

Maybe there were flashes of former selves. Friends, crushes, my atmospheric solitude. Our mother there but gone. And more—the potential of youth, its fullness. Did I find those ghosts or let them go? I wonder, still, who was the self I had expected Tom to help me become.

One year I sent him a gift package of cookies I made every Christmas. But several weeks later Dad said Tom had never come by, so he ended up eating them himself. After that, he told us there was no point in sending anything but cards. Tom could read our notes someday, he said, when he was getting better. Then he would know that we had been thinking of him all along. But my letters were awful—full of platitudes and stilted prose, tight with all I didn't say.

Mornings, Dad would scan the *Daily News* for bits about homeless men, reading close when a body was found in Chester Creek or Kincaid Park or somewhere else nearby, looking for the name: not Tom. He stopped taking trips during the winter, wanting always to be home to answer the door if Tom stopped by on a cold night.

Ignorance as a black hole, its event horizon limning every wintry hour.

There could be no Christmases, no Thanksgivings, no New Year's Eves without that thing. The wondering, the demands it made. Inside or outside, warm or cold, hungry or fed, desperate or content. His own birthday, late December. Family dinners, celebrations. There were no moments at all, really, without his absent body and the absent knowledge it signified.

·

People helped. His friends, my friends, family friends, neighbors, friends of friends. A teacher from our high school drew Tom indoors with the ruse that he needed someone to read aloud to, picking up *Moby-Dick,* keeping Tom listening as long as possible. A friend's parents left the outer door to their front vestibule unlocked when they were not home, so he could warm up in there anytime. A friend of Zach's, running into Tom on Spenard Road, gave him a pair of expensive fleece pants he happened to have with him.

The tension inside, whatever it was—always about to overtake me. I became a minor paranoiac, fretting over trivialities, my days pervaded by a sense of danger, ruled by panicky indecision. I stopped doing yoga, though I had practiced it off and on for years, finding the releases that came as I stretched and breathed too overwhelming. My heart would pound hard and my face would flush and I would feel dizzy and have to sit down. So instead I hiked, charging hard uphill, or I went out and laughed and drank and danced, or I closed myself in, watching DVDs alone in the dark, hour after hour.

Snow. Its faceted quality, the way it caught light, flashing at random angles as you moved. Frost. Rime. Hoar. Powder. Slush. Hail. Graupel. Névé.

Friends would say he came by their houses. They would say they ran into him at the library, they passed him in their cars. He was standing in the rain. He was in the parking lot beside Westchester Lagoon, staring off into space. They cooked him dinner or gave him a few bucks or let him take a shower. He was seen on C Street, on Fifth Avenue, or at a corner of the lagoon that we called the Ducks. They were worried, they were unsure what to do, they were impressed. *I* was impressed. Our friend Russell said to me, "In some ways I think of him as the ultimate Alaskan man."

I thought he was brave. I thought he was stupid. I thought he was smart. I thought he was stubborn. I knew, of course, that he was ill. When friends who saw him out walking asked me what they could do, I said, "Feed him."

Flake. Crystal. Bank. Drift. Cornice. Field. Glacier. Pack. Blizzard. Storm. Flurry. Shower. Slide. Burst. Avalanche. Crevasse.

Fear conflates the present with the past, makes one forget how to distinguish what has happened from what will happen yet. I have moments when, remembering those days, I feel a sudden pulse through my head and find myself wiping at tears. Then I register that it is a memory and as I catch my breath I hear myself saying, *It's over now. You don't ever have to feel that way again.*

All My Charms

IN MY FIFTH AND FINAL YEAR IN SANTA FE, I BEGAN BUILDing altars. Wiccan altars. All I can say is that I was feeling acutely aware of the forces that move the world, and of schizophrenia's role among those forces. Their power, their inevitability.

The altars were about all of that, but more specifically they were about objects—the detritus of lives lived and a planet turning, and the echoes I could catch in them. I found my objects on the ground, in the street, at trinket shops, or in the back corners of drawers and boxes. Forgotten articles I had once used were some of the best: a turquoise necklace I bought from a woman on the Plaza in Santa Fe, for instance, long before I ever lived there. Many were gifts: an amethyst necklace my brother gave me just as schizophrenia was overtaking him. He believed the stones were vibrating with miraculous energy. It was not the last gift he ever gave me, but like a fool I gave away the red sweater before I realized that was what it was.

SUN ALTAR FOR LITHA

Yellow napkin with scalloped edges

Blue silk scarf with design of a crane in flight

Large pillar candle

Disks: gold, mirrored

Turquoise necklace

Beaded neckband, broken

String of beads, pale green

Swiss Army watch, no band

Goose band stamped with the code ♥K2

Pintail feather

Blue faux-antique chalice, containing water

Bouquet of yellow roses

Green stone from a creek in Arizona

Red stone from a hill in New Mexico

Plastic figurine, tiger

When I made an altar, it was an improvisation. I would read about the Wiccan holiday at hand and think about what it meant. Once I had a feeling about what I needed to express, I dug around in my small dishes and boxes. Those lay about on dressers and desktops, decorative containers of lacquer or silk. Darting around looking for anything that felt right for what I was trying to say, I would sift through them and grab the things that spoke to me. Next I would build the framework of the altar: I'd choose a cloth, find a centerpiece, decide how many candles to use and where to place the incense. Then I started arranging objects.

Litha, for instance, is the longest day of the year, the summer solstice, when the days are warm and the sun is high. At Litha in 2011, when I looked at my mirrored disk (which I think was made to be a coaster), I thought of the scene in *Lawrence of Arabia* in which he had to cross the brutal section of desert known as the Sun's Anvil. In the middle of the disk I placed the plastic tiger figurine—my mother once sent it in the mail for no apparent reason—and felt that this represented me somehow. Then I thought the tiger needed a little help. So I placed the beaded band beneath him, and it seemed like a bridge across the no-man's-land. But the band was tied to another string of pale green beads, which made me think of life's soft beginnings, so I let that string lie in a loop at the end of the journey.

The other items fell into place after that. The scratched-up watch was a nod to the passage of time. The bird band and feather suggested the sky, as well as the place I got them from one summer, a part of Alaska where the sun never set. The bouquet of yellow roses, a gift from Will, I repurposed as a centerpiece. After nightfall, once the altar was in place, I held a ceremony and cast a spell that made use of the objects I had chosen.

CONTENTS OF WOODEN BOX
WITH RED HEART-SHAPED ROCK ON LID

Business card: Ditch Witch, Erika Wanenmacher

Packets of loose incense powders: Love, Come to
    Your Senses, Lighten the Load

Roll of extra-soft charcoal

Scented oils: anointing, Kyoto

Feathers: gray jay, parrot, peacock

Leaflet with instructions on how to use your spell, and a definition of magic:

> *Will is the deliberate, organized direction of intent toward a goal.*
>
> *Will works in partnership with imagination.*
>
> *Magic is the art of changing consciousness at will.*
>
> *Soooo, magic and spells work when clear intent is focused by will and imagination. . . .*
>
> *Have at it!*
>
> *Love, Erika*

I had rolled into witchcraft casually and was a little surprised by how well it stuck. It began while I was the arts editor at a magazine in Santa Fe, after one of my writers mentioned Erika Wanenmacher, the Ditch Witch—a local sculptor and multimedia artist who, he explained, was also a witch. She called herself a "culture witch" and thought of her artworks as magic spells—the means through which she could change the way people think, and thereby change the world.

I went to the gallery that displayed her work, stared at her impressively original sculptures—a black ceramic representation of herself, nude, with glass eyes embedded in the skin all over her body; a huge metallic marionette head with a screw coming out the top. I felt at once baffled and comforted by them. They seemed to break open the fabric of the world and stitch it back together as something more stubbornly visceral, weird and yet gentle. I thought of her artwork again that December when my friend Emily, who had never mentioned witchcraft to me before, told me she would be doing a Wiccan Yule ritual. I suppose it was why I said, "Oh, we should do it together."

Most Wiccan sabbats, or solar holidays, turned out to be familiar to me already. Ostara, the spring equinox, sounding so much like Easter. Samhain falling on Halloween. They are said to be based on European pagan holidays that were subsumed by the Church or lingered on in some other form. Yule, which falls on or around December 21, marks the winter solstice and was traditionally a night on which an enormous log was burned. In Emily's Yule ritual, we lit a smaller, symbolic log. She led me through the simple ceremony, first casting a magic circle around us and invoking the four elements, then lighting candles, explaining the significance of Yule, and calling for a short meditation. At that point, she asked me to name a dream or goal I wanted to set for myself for the coming year.

I could easily state one that was already in its infancy: move to New York, where I hoped to find a different way to write—a way into something more free-range than what I knew. I was also working my way out of my relationship with Will, who was an editor at another magazine, and with whom, it seemed clear one year in, I was already doomed. He was deeply ambivalent about us, and this was compounded by his habit of escaping into drink. Yet I was ruled by a precipitous kind of indecision when it came to him. Lately my life hadn't been moving forward in any other sense either. The move, I hoped, would bust me loose and launch a new phase of my life.

Soon I was finding templates for spells and ceremonies online, at Wiccan sites full of information about pagan traditions. I wasn't a careful student. I made altars and rituals almost without thought, winging it, throwing the elements together, letting the basic forms of the ceremonies and the items at hand determine the direction. Sometimes I would make changes on the fly. What came out always made more sense than I had intended. On bad days, when I was so stressed and frustrated I could barely think, I immersed myself entirely in my rituals. I began to notice that the worse I felt, the better my spells were. More original, focused, honest. I began to understand that something enormous was driving me, something subterranean that I couldn't name.

CONTENTS OF RUSSIAN LACQUER BOX WITH RABBIT LID

2008 quarter, state of Alaska design, grizzly bear with salmon

Silver pendant with star-shaped cutout

Pendant, crystals, shape of the letter *M*

Pin, shape of a panda

And so I began to symbolically act out my thoughts with my objects, arranging them, burning them, altering them. At its core the need was basic, the need for a way to acknowledge things that had long existed but remained unnamed, things that carried me back to my mother, to when she fell ill and took all of us through the looking glass with her—to when I had to learn how to figure out what was real on my own and decide for myself what I saw and believed. When I was eleven

I read Judy Blume's *Then Again, Maybe I Won't,* about a boy who has anxiety problems and whose doctor tells him he has a "nervous stomach." In a flash of insight, I understood that my chronic nausea was anxiety about my mother's worsening paranoia and the chaos it created in our lives. But my mother had a way of bluntly disagreeing with everything I said.

I told her, "Mom, I have a nervous stomach."

"Oh, pooh," she said. "No, you don't. Maybe you ate something."

I argued about it for a while, pointing out that it had been going on for months and that it wasn't a normal kind of feeling. I knew it got worse when she left town or tore my father's head out of all the family photos. But she wouldn't budge. This was the same summer she was checking in my ears to see if anyone had implanted a radio transmitter in my brain. She lived inside an elaborate set of delusions that flattened human beings into chess pawns and rendered little idiosyncratic me irrelevant or, worse, unreal. Often when I was talking to her I began to feel like a nonentity. She was so utterly unable to see me that sometimes I wondered if I was actually there.

I did not yet know the term *gaslighting,* the name for what was happening to me—that it comes from the 1944 film *Gaslight,* in which a man attempts to make his wife believe she is going mad by telling her everything she perceives is false. He turns down the gaslights, and when she comments that they're low he tells her no, they're the same as always. Then he turns them up and says the same thing. Of course my mother didn't gaslight me intentionally, but that didn't weaken its effect.

I coped by escaping. What I remember best about my mother's house is the time I spent outside of it, in our Anchorage cul-de-sac and an adjacent swath of state-owned forest—

floating on a pond in an inflatable rowboat, slapping water lilies with my oar, watching moose stroll through the black spruce on the far shore. Nature, which in Alaska was nearly everywhere. And science, which revealed the order within it. In my freshman year of high school, I read my entire biology textbook, even the chapters that were not assigned, just to see what it said. Just to know.

Twenty years later, I was still trying to make my world cohere. Living in the shadow of Tom's homelessness, I was often hit by the same terror of those early years, and when it came it took me to another place—one that I took to calling the Bad Place. Some event, a tiff with Will or bad news about Tom, would recall the old feelings and I'd fall into something like a flashback. It was more like reimmersion in a prior self. I was eleven years old again and I felt as I had felt then—that the floor of the world had fallen out from under me. I was like a scuba diver in turbid water, losing track of which way was up. It was pure, a kind of fear that usually only children feel, a fear not only of the loss of oneself or one's loved ones, but of the very structure of one's reality.

When this happened, I did whatever I could to get by until it eased up, passed over. And it was in those altered hours, when my mind was not rolling on its usual tracks, that I found myself picking up the objects in my home. A stone I had plucked from an Arizona river. A feather Will's son brought home from the park. I would roll them in my hands and between my fingers, and at the touch of them my skin would tingle and I would feel pulled back into myself a little bit. I'd become aware of my body again, a little more here and a little less back there. I'd begin to remember that I was going to be okay.

CONTENTS OF WHITE ENAMEL CUP

Two heart-shaped stones painted with nail polish, one maroon, one yellow

Ivory walrus tooth

Figurines, plastic: monkey holding a banana, tiger, golden baby, duckling, panda, pigeon sitting on a trash can

Figurine, glass: white rabbit with broken ear

Pendant, crystal snowflake

Figurine, ceramic: sleeping cat

Coins: Australian, platypus; American, Sacagawea; Mexican, eagle with snake and cactus

Oval rabies tag, heavily worn

Pin with logo for Taos Coyotes hockey team

Amethyst, two chunks

This was the year I practiced Wicca diligently, marking every sabbat with an altar and a ritual, making use of the moon to cast regular spells. Officially, Wicca acknowledges a higher power, and nearly all other witches I have come across believe in some type of deity—making me, an atheist witch, a bit of an oddball. But a spell is not a prayer, and for me the craft was never about a higher power. I was in it for the practice, for the repeated act of interpreting my life through its shrapnel, and for the way this forced me to examine and evaluate that life. I was not asking some greater force to change the world for me. I was changing it for myself.

CONTENTS OF SILK BOX
WITH EMBROIDERED CHINESE SYMBOL

Six rings: three silver, three gold

Charm bracelet with six charms: megaphone, cross,
    heart, ulu, crescent moon, key

I collected my objects haphazardly. I would buy the ones
I needed for particular functions—candles, small plates,
incense—but the rest I preferred to find, to feel that they had
come to me. "This is so witchy," I'd say of a trinket, and put it
in my pocket. Most of the items I used were given to me—gifts
or small knickknacks left in my car by road-tripping friends,
boyfriends, sisters. One, a strange fragment of rusty iron, actually fell out of the sky and landed on my windowsill. Many
were remnants of my childhood before my mother became ill,
chance survivors of her repeated purges of possessions, which
took place periodically until she had no possessions left.

Who knows how the charm bracelet she gave me when I
was four, to which we added a charm every birthday until I
was ten, has stayed with me. I don't remember what kept it
safe and close through all these years. I hardly noticed it until
it occurred to me that it was perfect spell-casting material—
and I was struck by the use of the word *charm*. The charm
bracelet: a kind of spell, a string of talismans for love, success,
protection. In some sense I suppose that's what my mother
meant it to be.

My mother has always been a keeper of small boxes and an
appreciator of things miniature. In my childhood she had them
around on side tables, piano tops, window ledges, wherever. I

never consciously imitated her, but as I grew up I found that I had my own collection of small boxes too, and I needed them because I had things to put in them. Rings I no longer wore but loved too sentimentally to give away. Coins from foreign countries, too pretty to hand off. The broken arrowhead one boyfriend gave me, the nautilus fossil I bought from a camel-trek guide on the trip I took to Morocco with my sister. My "cauldron" was actually a ceramic drinking-chocolate bowl a friend brought back from Oaxaca, which I kept half filled with dirt.

For years I accumulated small objects—things that I found I could never let go when I cleaned out my car or packed up my room to move again. In that time, I lived in six different states and traveled to the Mediterranean, the Sahara, the Himalaya, the Galápagos, the Great Barrier Reef. Deserts, jungles, oceans, glaciers. I knew I'd never be back on the Yukon Delta, where rotting walrus carcasses were part of the scenery. I'd never again see my first boyfriend, who gave me my first heart-shaped rock, picked up from a beach in Chile.

But more than that, what gave my objects their power was that I was once a teenage girl who could find no words for her own life. Who had been unable to speak of her family's suffering. That I was once a woman in her twenties who watched her brother fall, as her mother had, to schizophrenia. Who, when words failed a second time, turned to colors and shapes and sounds, dyeing her hair blue and playing guitar in rainbow-striped pants and thick black eyeliner and a T-shirt emblazoned with the word *asylum*.

There is always something that comes before words, before I find the words, and it is in that place that my stones and trinkets and broken pieces have meant everything. I've had them when words failed me, escaped me, betrayed me, misconstrued me, or erased me. I created my own language from these objects, each one a slippery signifier with meanings and resonances that only I knew. And when I made an altar I could build a web of meanings around things too inchoate or painful or frightening to speak. This was the edge of language, and I used it when I found myself at the edge of my world, carried there by schizophrenia. These objects anchored me to my life when I forgot again that I was real, that anything was real. When the scaffold of the world collapsed, leaving only madness and more madness. These were the fragments I shored against my ruin.

CONTENTS OF VINTAGE *ALASKA: THE LAST FRONTIER* PORCELAIN TRAY

Chunk of myrrh

Pendant, resin, Tlingit wolf design

Chambered nautilus fossil

Necklace of small turquoise beads

Flat gray pebble

Figurine, ceramic, very old: cat playing with yarn

If altar building was an act that occurred before language, spell casting happened at the point where language began. It was through language that I, as both a witch and a writer, would reclaim some control over the shadowy monsters in my mind—those unconscious memories, those black fears. Spells, many say, will not work unless the spell caster focuses her intent into words, preferably rhymes. These must be either stated aloud or written down. (Rhyme, according to the Wiccan Rede, binds the spell, so I indulged in writing whole verses of bad poetry—all of it so wretched that I'm too embarrassed to repeat any here.) The use of words in spells is a common requirement that to me feels fundamental to witchcraft. It seems, too, somehow fundamental to humanity. "In the beginning," reads the Gospel of John, "was the Word, and the Word was with God, and the Word was God."

A spell, in the simplest sense, is a ritual in which a person expresses her intention while symbolically enacting the desired result. For me, spell casting was about focusing my mind and staying present with what I wanted. For a Letting Go spell, for instance, I might toss something into a fire and save the ashes. The spell would then be contained in the ashes, which I would keep close by. I read that the best time for spell casting is during an esbat—a full moon—or at any moon phase that seemed appropriate to my goal. So I'd cast Getting Over a Broken Heart on a waning moon; Finding My Way on a new moon. I would eventually see that I needed witchcraft because it suggested some way to project myself into the future. Because I had never understood how to have a relationship to things that didn't yet exist. But the most important spell I ever encountered was not my own.

This was how witchcraft became an obsession during the months preceding my move to New York. My involvement with Will had begun the previous summer with highest hopes but fell to earth six months in. He had at first seemed an antidote to my past troubles, and at times he was the most soothing presence in my life. But that was a lot to ask of one person, especially given that he had a drinking problem and a divorce so fresh that it wasn't finalized until after we started dating. He wanted to be with me, then he wasn't sure, then he wanted to be with me as long as that didn't involve too much being with me. We settled into a cycle of coming together and slipping apart, which triggered my old fears and sent me often to the Bad Place. By February I was sure we were hopeless, but I was cripplingly in love. I cast spell after spell, taking advantage of any opportunity to conjure some Personal Power, Guidance, or Letting Go. By summer, after trying and failing to dump him twice, I couldn't wait to get farther away. There was no question that he wouldn't come to New York with me. He had a job and two kids.

Around that time, someone told me about the Ditch Witch store. Erika Wanenmacher had opened a shop. I knew from her artist statement for her previous year's show that every day she walked her dog on a path that followed the Acequia Madre—the Mother Ditch, Santa Fe's centuries-old irrigation canal that runs through the oldest part of town. On her walks, she found all kinds of items on the ground—lighters, bent spoons, bits of porcelain, rusty tools, weatherworn liquor bottles. She collected the ones that appealed to her and took them back to her studio, where she used them to make her own style of spell. She would select a few objects, rim them in silver so they suggested stained glass, solder small hoops to them, and then tie them together on strands of black twine so they hung as long clusters on the wall. Her spells were sculptures.

A dozen or so of these were hanging on the wall when I stopped by the shop. It was just a corner space she rented within a larger store that sold art glass, and it was lined with shelves loaded with candles, incense, and items pulled from the ditch. Erika was out, but the glass store owner explained the spells, saying, "She does custom spells too. You can ask her to make you one if none of these are what you need."

Time folded in on itself that summer. I was freelancing as an art critic, and when Erika had a gallery show I reviewed it in my column. At her opening I saw her but was too shy to walk up and say hello. Meanwhile, though I wanted things to work out with Will, I was giving up on him, preparing to leave, getting things done by just forcing myself to not stop moving. Fill these boxes. Buy this packing tape. Visit this art show. Will said he didn't know if he was in love with me. I told him he was a fool. I was living on hubris and a determination to not let my friends see what sorry shape I was in. I started selling off my stuff, winnowing my possessions down to necessities and what fit in my little boxes. In a weird twist, the guy who showed up to buy my bike was Will's ex-wife's new boyfriend. He wanted to give it to her as a gift. Stunned, I told him that was fine with me. Gone. Done.

Earlier that summer, finches had flown into the storage room in the house I shared with my roommate and nested in the hanging plant beside my bathroom window. Every day I would sneak up and stand on the toilet to see the baby birds in their nest. After they fledged I stared at the empty nest for weeks, full of angst. Then one day I took it down and set it in a corner of my room, and as I sorted my stuff and prepared to move, whenever I came across some small scrap of paper or other piece of detritus, I tossed it in the nest. This would be my last Santa Fe spell—Taking Flight. On a night lit by a waxing moon in late July, in Adrienne's yard, we set the nest inside a big fireproof bowl and lit it on fire, and then I jumped over it as it burned. Goodbye, Santa Fe. Goodbye, Will.

MOON ALTAR FOR TAKING FLIGHT SPELL

Sky-blue tissue paper

House finch nest

Found paper scraps

Three pillar candles

Four elements: pile of dirt (earth), feather (air), red
     candle (fire), cup of water

Moon disks: mirrored, mother-of-pearl, silver

Feathers

Necklace of turquoise beads

White handkerchief

I called Erika and said I wanted to buy a custom spell. We set
up a time to meet at the Ditch Witch store. She was a rect-
angular woman in a tank top and worn jeans, with cropped
hair, a thick nose, and tattoos of flowers and birds winding up
her arms and shoulders. When I walked in she started talking
and didn't stop.

"The word *witch* comes from the Old English *wych*," she
said. "W-Y-C-H. It means 'to bend.' What I do is try to bend
people's perceptions, just a little bit." She gestured as if bending the air in front of her, as if it gave resistance and she had
to really tweak it. She didn't make much eye contact with me,
and her manner had the geekiness of a computer program-
mer. I suspected that, similarly, she was used to spending her
time translating what appeared to be a near-constant stream
of thoughts into code—some personal lexicon by which she
sorted her universe and rendered it as art.

"I'm moving to New York," I said. "I need a spell for a soft
landing." I paused. It was time to put the rest into words. As
I had done when I first began saying *schizophrenia* out loud,
and then cried at random times for months while it sunk in
that refusing to say it hadn't made it disappear. Now would

be the time to turn away from that chaos, that inaccessibility. "And—I want a partner," I said, "someone who wants to build a life with me."

She wrote my words down and looked at a cabinet behind her, which was full of old boxes and worn bottles and bowls full of amulets. "I think I know where I can start," she said.

When I came back for the finished spell, she had it inside a refurbished wooden box onto which she had glued a red heart-shaped rock. She held up the glinting spell and explained each of the items, all of which came from the ditch. A red porcelain shard meant love. A large heart-shaped rock was me and a small one was the partner I would find. A pencil and slate she put there because, as a writer, I might want to write something of my own onto the spell. "Hang it up near you, someplace where you'll see it a lot," she said. "And read what it says on the flyer. Magic is the art of changing consciousness at will."

CONTENTS OF ERIKA'S CUSTOM SPELL

Clear glass lid, no handle

Coat hook, bent, rusty

Copper disk with a pentagram painted on one side and LOVE, ERIKA 2010 on the other

Glass bottle with cork lid, filled with dirt, incense, and blue "magic sand"

Shard of blue-glazed stoneware

Shard of red-glazed porcelain

Shard of green-glazed stoneware

Shard of white porcelain with red deciduous-tree
   design

Large heart-shaped rock

Small heart-shaped rock

Short yellow pencil

Flat piece of slate

Thin copper tag hand-engraved with words
   articulating the spell:

Marin
Partner in All Aspects
Soft Landing

I have an idea that love is less a feeling than an action, or really
a long series of actions that intertwine to form a kind of web,
and the web is life. I perform acts of love for the people I love,
and so create my world. In the same way, witchcraft isn't a
system of belief for me so much as it is a series of acts—of
imagination and will. These are the acts by which I have built
a life where madness does not reign.

When I took home Erika's spell I didn't mention it to Will.
He knew I had ordered one, but I never told him what I asked
for. He seemed in a state of suspension, behaving as if we
would be together forever and yet as if we were not together
at all. "Once I'm gone," I told him, "it's over, you know. For
good. I can't ever come back to this."

"Yes," he said gravely, "I know." But something in his face
made me suspect it wasn't sinking in.

One week after I got to New York, I told him I needed to
stop the phone calls for a while. Okay, he said. My landing, it

turned out, was blissfully soft. In my new apartment I hung the spell on the wall above my bed. I took a look at online dating, and on Facebook I changed my relationship status to *single*.

That did it. I marvel that what it took to convince a forty-four-year-old man that I was actually breaking up with him was a change in status on Facebook. But it hit him like a train. Three days later he wanted me back. No, I said. On one side of the slate I wrote, "Someone who wants to build a life with me."

No, I said, and I kept saying it. He kept calling. He'd had an epiphany, he said. "It's too late," I said. He would repeat himself, and I would say I'd wait and see. I told him this would never work unless he took control of his life. Regularly I glanced at my spell, fiddled with its pieces, reminded myself that I believed in what it represented, that such a partner must exist and be capable of being found. Something about the spell's own objecthood, its concreteness, made that imagined future seem more probable. Even likely. It could be touched. On the other side of the slate I wrote, "Someone who can lead. Someone who knows himself." And at night I sighed in relief for the many miles that kept me from driving to his house and climbing into his bed.

We went on like this. As we talked I would lie on my bed and look up at my spell. One night as we Skyped I showed it to him, and read him its tag, and read what I had written on the slate. He looked as sad as I had ever seen him.

When he quit drinking, I was floored. Then he came up with a plan to leave his editing job and split his time between New York and the Southwest, working as a freelancer. He said he could make it work. It seemed that the determined, devoted man I had once seen in him had returned. And become more.

"Who are you and what have you done with my boyfriend?" I said.

"This *is* me," he replied. "This is me being me." He told me he wanted to be the small rock in my spell. I said that if we were going to try again, we needed to work through all the things that had gone wrong that first year. He agreed.

That spring we hung the spell up in our new Manhattan apartment, inside an old gold-leaf frame my grandmother once gave me. And when we later moved to Tucson together, I gave it pride of place in our new house. It would be glib to say the spell worked. I worked. Will worked. The world remained as wild as ever, of course. But we found a new way to do things, the two of us, by way of that spell. So sometimes I still pause beside the wall where it now hangs, and I touch the red porcelain. Sometimes I take the slate in my fingers and turn it so the graphite catches light from the window, and I read again the magic words.

Vagabond

WHEN YOU GO HUNTING FOR ADVICE ABOUT HOW TO HELP a mentally ill loved one, much of what you find actually focuses on what you can do for yourself: Learn as much as you can about mental illness, find a supportive community, ask questions. We did this, all of us. We took the National Alliance on Mental Illness's free classes. We read books like *When Madness Comes Home* and *Surviving Schizophrenia*. I talked to doctors and read articles and met with support groups. Dad consulted experts, conferred with lawyers, met with people with schizophrenia who had rebuilt their lives. He even gave presentations at the police department to help Crisis Intervention Team–trained officers better understand mental illness and its human costs. Much of this helped us enormously, and it certainly improved my relationship with my mother, but ultimately it did very little for Tom.

I had had it in my head that it would take maybe six months or a year on the street before Tom changed his mind about treatment. It was a number I pulled out of the air and soon enough it was proven wrong. I did continue to believe that eventually, with us or without us, Tom would choose to come inside again and begin the long, slow journey back to health. But I must have known the odds deep down, held them there, buried: the likelihood of things going another way. His thoughts were so convoluted, his grasp on reality so thin. What drove his decisions was at once more immediate and far more distant than such a choice required. He was aware of the basest necessities and most transcendent abstractions, and almost nothing in between. All the midlevel motivations—for applying for jobs and signing a lease and paying bills and buying towels and mopping the floor and changing the oil—all that had fallen away.

As I learned more about schizophrenia, I would call Dad and offer up suggestions, wondering could we try this, could we try that. But inevitably he had already considered and discarded the ideas. *Could we get him an apartment? Pay the rent and utilities for him?* He'd leave something on the stove and burn the place down. *What about hiring a personal caregiver?* They couldn't be there twenty-four hours a day. That would take three full-time employees. *What about API?* API didn't have enough beds to meet the demand, so it pushed people out as quickly as possible. *What about a private psychiatric hospital, someplace he could stay longer—like the place Mom was at for three months?* Charter North was no longer a psych hospital but an addiction recovery center for teens. *What about some other private psych hospital?* There were no other psych hospitals in Alaska, private or otherwise. *What about moving him to a hospital outside of Alaska?* He'd walk away. We couldn't force him to stay there, and once he was out he could go anywhere. We'd never see him again.

I thought of Tom out there in the enormity of America,

unknown in the communities he passed through, uncared for, with no one around to look out for him, no one to tell us they had spotted him, no way for Dad to check on him. Places where the cops didn't have CIT training, where police were more aggressive toward people with mental illness than they were in Anchorage. I had begun noticing news items about police killings of unarmed or lightly armed mentally ill men in situations that could have been de-escalated. It was common enough if you kept an eye out for it. And in my conversations with others who had mental illness in their families, I had heard about parents who avoided calling the cops when an ill son was unstable because they were afraid he'd be shot rather than helped. No. That didn't seem like the best idea.

In wild, fleeting moments I considered moving back to Anchorage, to work at a café and rent a place downtown and spend my free time convincing Tom to come back inside. I knew, we all knew, that Adrienne or I could try this, but I balked when I considered what it meant. I had seen enough of Tom's schizophrenia to not expect my efforts to make a difference, though now that sentiment feels like an excuse. But I also worried for myself. Depression stalked me, coming on thick every winter despite my efforts to find a helpful antidepressant, as did the terrible tension. I was afraid that as soon as I got to Anchorage, the muscles in my back would knot up, as they always did now when I thought much about Tom, and with this would come the crushing feeling and the strange stillness, and I would be no help at all. Things were not so different for Adrienne. And we both knew that Dad would not want us to do it. In general, he preferred to handle things on his own, but we knew he also wanted to protect us. "Tom already has no life," he said sometimes. "I don't want you girls to have no life either."

Sean consoled me by saying that, in his experience, mental illness tended to be harder on the sufferer's loved ones than on the sufferer himself. But I never knew how fully his own experience could apply to Tom, and I wondered if he was exaggerating a bit in order to make me feel better. It did appear that Tom's situation bothered Tom much less than it bothered the rest of us, and I suppose there was solace in that—however much his contentment may have hinged on being unable to grasp how much he had lost, unable to care that he had lost it, and unable to believe he would receive so little in return.

We could visit, at least, but none of us sisters had the money to fly home very often. I might have asked Dad to pay, but as a rule I avoided asking him for things. And my sisters, who had more contentious relationships with him, could not have asked. That was the way of things. Tom's schizophrenia didn't occur in a vacuum. It occurred within our family—a family that had already been shaped by loss and mental illness, a family that was barely functional even at its best.

Dad found many small ways to help, but he was largely at sea, often failing to grasp how Tom's mind had been changed by illness. Others sometimes tried to help too, but found it no easier. Zach took on a larger role than most, regularly letting Tom crash at his house. Other times, he offered food or listened while Tom rambled. But he often left town for work, so his efforts were fraught with complications. Once, when he was away for a few days with Tom at the cabin he was renting, Tom left a candle burning on a wooden windowsill and Zach came home to find it blackened and charred. It was just luck that the whole place didn't go up in flames.

Another high school friend, Russell, who had his own story of psychosis and jail and hospitalization, whose illness had much in common with Tom's, took an interest in him and made efforts to connect with him whenever he could, stopping to talk, asking how he was, offering what he had. Russell was earning a degree in computer science at UAA, and in time he became like a beacon to me, his successes pointing me toward an idea of what kind of life Tom might someday have for himself. In the meantime, Russell would send us photographs and updates—Tom in matted dreadlocks, Tom midsentence, Tom with an awkward smile. Russell once remarked to Adrienne that Tom was always happy. "No," she said, "I think it's you. I think he likes you."

It worked out best, though, with Sean and Kevin. Only they seemed to have the perfect touch—perhaps because Sean, with his bipolar disorder, understood hospitalization and medication from experience, and yet also had some distance from the worst of it. Tom would show up at their house, hungry and depleted, and end up camping in their living room for weeks on end, lounging on the couch while they were at work and then crashing on it at night. In his first few days there he could consume mountains of food, throwing back a gallon of milk and thousands of calories daily. And like young parents, they would coordinate runs to the grocery store to make sure there was always enough for him. They were our surrogates and our saviors, feeding him, keeping him company, keeping him warm. In their casual, easygoing way, they took better care of him than anyone but Dad ever would.

But not even Sean could change his mind about treatment. Tom didn't like to talk about medication and would get cranky if anyone brought it up, and if Sean mentioned it too many times, Tom would move on from their living room and they wouldn't see him again for a while. Meanwhile, Tom's life was an exercise in futility. He was focused on a plan to swim across the Pacific Ocean to Japan, embarking on a training regimen that entailed standing, fully clothed, in Sean and Kevin's shower with the cold water running for hours at a time. Day after day he did this, and since it was in their only bathroom, Kevin's girlfriend, Raina, had to sometimes sneak in to use the toilet in secret. But they didn't make him stop. I think they loved him for it.

And when Alicia flew home with her infant son but was unable to find him, it was Kevin who called her on her very last day and said, "Your brother's at my house." So she arrived to find Tom in his knit wool cap with his pack full of rocks, and she held her baby up toward him, saying, "Tom, this is your nephew." And Kevin pulled out his camera and started snapping shots—there was Tom smiling softly, showing the baby a rock. There was Tom peering at the questing infant eyes, enchanted by the tiny hand that gripped his finger.

How can I convey the quality of their love? Years later, at Tom's memorial, Kevin would retell the story of how Tom took over the shower, laughing as he remembered it. And Raina, nodding, would act out for us how she crept in to pee, watching the shower curtain, trying to hurry. And soon we would all be laughing—laughing with Kevin even as he began to cry, as he cried on through his laughter, laughing through his tears, shaking his head, saying, "Swimming to Japan."

I made it home at last in 2009—nearly three years into Tom's time of homelessness. It was June, the lightest, warmest time of year. Flying in from Santa Fe on a clear evening, I got a view of the southern mountains, massive tangles of peaks and glaciers sprawling across the landscape. In my window seat with my face pressed to the glass, I cried from homesickness. When we landed I felt my belonging the moment I stepped outside, as if in my cells. Something of the cool air, its moisture, its smell. The blue dusk. The ridge of the Chugach guarding the city like a great wall.

My goal with Tom, if I conceived it as such, was to glimpse a way to get through to him, to spot an opening to convince him to come inside and get help. But I wasn't very strategic about it. I had no actual plan, no idea what my plan should look like if I did. What I wanted most pressingly was just to see him—to be reminded that he was real, and maybe remember again that he was mine.

The only way to find him was to go searching the streets. I put word out that if anyone spotted him or knew where he hung out, I'd like to know. Sean told me he believed he was camping out, but also that he was secretive about it and wouldn't say where. For two days I did little more than drive around scanning the sidewalks, searching for the figure of him walking. I kept thinking I saw him, only to discover it was someone else. It made me feel a little insane, the acuteness of his nearness, the chance of driving right past him without noticing.

Finally, early one afternoon, Dad got a call from his friend Bruce, who said, "I'm looking at Tom right now." We sprang up and drove to the intersection where Bruce had pulled over, keeping Tom in his sight, still on the phone. Dad handed me some cash, reminded me to ask Tom if he wanted some new clothes, and said, "See if you can get him to come by the house." At the intersection, waiting for the light to change, I spotted Tom getting up from a bench and ran across the four-lane throughway to reach him.

As I approached, he didn't initially turn. "Hi, Tom," I said to get his attention, unsure if he had seen me yet. My eyes were already welling up. Glancing my way, he replied, "Have you figured out I'm your brother yet?"

He wore a heavy gray wool cap and a fisherman's cardigan over a black zip-up turtleneck, his face ruddy from the constant summer daylight, with a wispy red beard that wandered out in all directions. His fingernails were long, with dark ridges of dirt beneath them, and his teeth had yellowed deeply. I noticed how thin he was, bonier than I had ever thought his dense frame would be. He still wasn't looking at me directly, and for a moment I just stood there, taking him in, trying to keep my tears quiet, thinking maybe he wouldn't notice them. But then he stood and flashed me a look and said, "Yeah, times are hard all around."

Across the intersection stood the long, low strip mall that housed Anchorage's giant REI store, as well as a sandwich shop where we had often eaten in years past. Thinking to feed him, I asked Tom if he wanted to go there. After a brief hesitation, he agreed. But it wasn't a good idea. It was loud and crowded in there, the lunch rush, and as we waited in line to order food a faint look of distress grew on his face. Then he resisted my offer to buy him lunch. I finally talked him into getting a sandwich and promised we could go sit out on the patio, and he visibly calmed once we stepped outside. Then, as I ate, he started talking—a long, low monotone stream of ideas, a nearly unceasing flow that caught me and brought me right up to the fluid edge of his world.

He spoke not to me so much as at me, not noticing that I couldn't hear much over the traffic noise. He shifted amorphously from topic to topic, circling back, digressing, repeating, skipping out, fading in, every subject coming up apropos of nothing. He talked of Catholic priests and the samurai code and a new kind of education system for which he was designing the textbooks. I could hear the schizophrenia in his speech—the "clanging." Sometimes he would repeat a word or pause to spell it, or follow it with words that rhymed or assonated, his sentences progressing via not meaning but sound. I struggled to follow without getting bogged down in his involuted language, a little bit stunned by the earnest ambition fueling his chaotic thoughts.

Eventually even the activity on the patio started to bother him, so I suggested we go. "I could just walk along with you for a while," I said, "until you don't want to anymore." He stared at me a moment and then agreed. So we walked and he talked, heading out across the parking lot and down Northern Lights Boulevard toward Carrs grocery store, and then across the street to thread around our old junior high and high schools. And as we passed under the tall wall of the West High Auditorium, with its giant mural of a bald eagle reaching for an anchor, Tom digressed midsentence to say, "West, W-E-S-T." And I wondered what of those memories hung in his heart as they hung in mine.

Turning onto a bike path, I saw in Tom's eyes a vulnerable kind of uncertainty that I had never seen in them before. It was faint but clear, a hesitant look that I had often seen on our mother's face and that seemed somehow part of schizophrenia. It was unnerving—how unprotected he and Mom could appear, as if they lacked the psychic shields that the rest of us wore always. I felt, too, his paranoia. Suspicion hovered around us, in the background, at every moment. Occasionally he eyed me sidelong as if to size me up or catch me out, seeming torn between politeness and mistrust, affection and self-preservation. In the selfie I took, his face was intent, distracted by a thought, his stance guarded. Though he pressed in for the photo, his shoulders were hunched. And as if to highlight the contrast, the camera caught my own perfect on-demand smile beside him. It was instead my body that gave me away, leaning toward him so eagerly that my hoop earring swung awkwardly outward.

For over an hour we wandered through the woods around downtown, following the bike paths around Westchester Lagoon and then into the alders and spruces that lined Chester Creek, and eventually up a long hill that gave us a view. When I asked Tom how often he saw Dad, a shadow fell over his face and he began to ruminate, calling Dad by his full name, as if he were a stranger or a public figure. He was still angry—that was clear. But his thoughts were garbled, and I suspected that he no longer remembered much about what had happened between them, only that his father had turned him away. I felt a wave pass through me, sickly and unsteadying, as I registered that the message behind Dad's decision had been lost.

Then I brought up Mom and Adrienne and watched his eyes turn gentle, fond of the thought of them, before he slipped back into his default look of confused concentration. I asked if he needed any camping gear. A tent, a tarp, a sleeping bag. He said no. I asked where he camped, if it was in these woods somewhere, but he ignored the question. I tried to give him the twenties Dad had handed me, but he wouldn't look at them. I suggested that he come by the house while I was visiting, for dinner and a shower and some new clothes. But he shook his head. I was getting nowhere. And yet I felt that he was giving me everything. Everything he could find within himself to offer up. It was thirty years' worth of love and madness distilled into a single summer hour.

And this was when he paused in our progress up the hill and quietly demanded, "Do you remember the time you tried to kill me?"

Abashed, I took a long time to reply. I had, he told me, come after him in a crowd with a pistol. We all had, the whole family. I had shot at him. Now he waited. "No, I don't remember that," I finally said. And then, finding my footing, "I didn't do that." But I couldn't tell what he made of this, if he accepted the denial.

At the top of the hill, he faced me and said this was enough talking. Reluctantly I nodded and held out the bag containing the uneaten half of his sandwich. He took it absently.

And then, after I let out a few obvious phrases—*Okay I love you nice to see you thanks for the walk*—and again shoved some bills at him and was surprised when he took them, he turned back down the hill, rounded a bend, and was gone.

Animate

THE STORY GOES THAT MARIO IS LUIGI'S BROTHER. NEARLY all we know about him is that he is a brother. We also know that he wears red and Luigi wears green. It is easy to infer that they must be close, having gone into the same line of work (plumbing) and being the title characters of the same video game (*Super Mario Bros.*).

I see us from behind, the backs of our heads, three in a row on chairs pulled close in front of the television. Adrienne, the blonde. Tom, the youngest. And me. Ignoring our mother when she ignores us, unable to hear beyond the voices in her head. Turning to this other place inside the television, to the freedom of its two-dimensional universe. I have the gray rectangle of the Nintendo controller in my hands. Hands on buttons, they stay that way for five years. The houses change, the rooms change, the TV grows and shrinks and turns color as one model is swapped out for another. The games change too, but Mario is the hinge on which all the rest hang, the alternate reality that cleaves us to the idea of alternate realities.

.

When you play the game, Mario becomes a sort of doppel-gänger, enacting your thoughts in his block-and-pixel world. When you punch (button A), he punches. When you run (button B), he runs. You live his adventures along with him, and yet you are never quite inside them. You see him only and always in profile. He is linked to you and yet he is not you. So it is with brothers. Mine sat beside me year after year, face to the screen, eyes on the action. (Disregarding the foil balls our mother placed on the antennae, disregarding her warnings about cosmic rays.) Telling me which brick to punch to get the secret fire flower, or the vine that unfurls up into clouds and golden coins. Outgrowing his shoes, saving the princess, outwitting the games—version 2, version 3. One day his hands were bigger than mine.

In Mario's world, the straight line of his horizon extends ever to the right, while what is behind him to the left vanishes with each step he takes forward. Mario's past is forever irretrievable. If he turns to go back, the edge of the screen refuses to give way. This is also the case with me, as I will learn. I will learn, as I grow taller (as Mario grows taller when he finds a giant mushroom)—I will learn, as I reach the prime of youth and taste invincibility (as Mario becomes invincible when he captures a flashing star)—I will learn that turning back to the left and returning to the castle at the end of the previous level (the one in which Mario threw fireballs at the tortoise-dragon until it fell through its drawbridge into red lava) is impossible.

This does not at first seem to be the case. It seems that in my memory I can travel anywhere I have ever been. I can conjure those brothers and my own with ease. I can sense the shape of Tom's fingers and the quality of his inward gaze, and I can feel madness like a ghost in the walls. But then comes the day when I wish to go back, to truly go back, not just to approximate that last castle but to inhabit it again. The moment comes when I hurl my cellphone down onto the bed and watch it bounce to the floor, and I find myself thinking that we must rewind this, we must return to the previous moment. The moment happens when I call Will and when he asks what's up I say, "No no no no no no no no no."

It has occurred to me that *life* is not the existence of a body in space but its movements within space. An animal that is animate is one that is alive. Every cell is engaged in the flow of molecules within and between the tissues, and without that movement a creature is dead. I thought about this as I imagined my brother, post-autopsy (required, confirming the suicide), lying on a shelf in a freezer that I could not visit to see him one last time. So I zoomed in close in my thoughts, trying to catch again the curve of his jaw, the width of his nose. I zoomed all the way down into his cells, where I saw that no proton pumps churned ions across membranes. No ribosomes dutifully transcribed RNA into proteins. No neurons pulsed electrical signals. Never had a stillness been more complete.

The thing about the game is that when Mario dies it is you who decides what happens next. As in life, you do not die with him. You remain young and strong and fully composed of flesh and bone and sinew. But then you press the Start button and he appears again. As before. And you go on, and you begin to believe in endless second chances. That in every way the logic of the game will reach beyond the screen. That there will always be another opportunity for your pain, for your brother's pain, to be redeemed.

Vagabond

THINGS HAD CHANGED, MYSTERIOUSLY AND SUDDENLY. IN 2009, as winter crept in, Tom set up a camp for himself under a boat in the yard across the street from Dad's house. It was a fairly large wooded lot that bordered on a small creek, and amid the trees there was an old wooden fishing boat stored upright under a large blue tarp. Tom established himself beneath it, in the sheltered space between the tarp and the hull.

Later, when I learned of this, I felt that Tom's circumstances had never seemed more unreal. Under a boat. It was a phrase everyone repeated, as if it meant something. He wasn't just living in a yard directly across from Dad's house, but also under a boat. We kept saying it. As if by holding up the phrase and turning it, by passing it around almost as a talisman, we might use it to catch the light and discern the meaning of what was happening. This was the way things changed with schizophrenia—jarringly, seemingly without preamble, leaving you to wonder what you missed and forcing you to conclude that you missed everything.

.

Dad had last seen Tom one evening when he stopped by the house, not long after Halloween. Excited, Dad washed his clothes and convinced him to take a shower and wash his hair a few times, and he gave him a haircut and some new clothes. They went out to dinner. Things went well, and although Tom was "pretty out there," Dad wrote, he seemed "neither worried nor unhappy." Dad brought up the question of where Tom could live for the winter, but Tom said he had lots of places to stay, and when Dad tried to give him a hundred dollars, he would only take twenty. It wasn't yet apparent that something was getting worse for Tom, his mind on the verge of spinning into darker places.

Sometime later, Dad learned that Tom was under the boat across the street and had been living there for a few weeks. The neighbors had known Tom since he was a little boy and had always liked him, so they said they didn't mind it. At first, Dad let it be. The spot under the boat was quiet and safe. But eventually it got very cold, and Dad, worrying, went to see if Tom was okay. Tom lashed out, raging at Dad for coming over and poking around, shouting repeatedly to go away, stay away. Stunned, Dad backed off and didn't bother him again.

Around that time, Zach was living in a house nearby with an unused bedroom and convinced his roommates to let Tom live there rent-free. Though Tom was more agitated than usual that winter, he at first seemed content, just quietly hanging out in the bedroom they gave him. But soon there was friction with one of the roommates, and then when they learned that the owners were going to sell the house, Tom began to believe that he had bought it. Things came to a head one day when Tom was home alone and took the only key, locking the roommate out of the house. (It was Dad who finally got the key back, calling Zach's house and inviting Tom to dinner, offering to wash his clothes, and then digging through the pockets to find it.) Zach had to tell Tom he could no longer live there. Soon he was back under the boat.

In early spring, after a few weeks of increasingly erratic behavior, Tom started ranting and screaming obscenities at the neighbors who owned the boat. Dad had gone to Girdwood for the weekend and so wasn't there to step in. The neighbors, alarmed, called the police, and when the cops arrived, Tom asked to be taken to API. This was, as far as we knew, the first time he had ever actively sought psychiatric care.

ALASKA PSYCHIATRIC INSTITUTE
Admission Psychiatric Evaluation
Admission Date: 04/14/10

IDENTIFYING DATA: This is the second Alaska Psychiatric Institute (API) admission for this 32-year-old unmarried Caucasian male. Past psychiatric evaluation indicates the patient is college educated, at one point achieving a 3.9 grade point average until onset of psychotic symptoms.

PRESENTING PROBLEM/CHIEF COMPLAINT: The patient was referred to the Alaska Psychiatric Institute from the Psychiatric Emergency Department at Providence Alaska Medical Center for evaluation of psychosis. The patient was floridly psychotic during this interview but appeared to be making a good-faith effort to be cooperative with assessment and interventions.

HISTORY OF PRESENT ILLNESS: The patient has a history of schizophrenia. Apparently, he has been living under a boat in the neighbor's yard. Providence reports that the patient was seen hallucinating and was threatening to kill his neighbor. His neighbor was scared and no longer wants the patient to live on his property. The patient arrived to Providence wearing a shirt that was full of burn holes from cigarettes. The patient was loud, disorganized, and threatening. He was held in psychiatric observation and given Zyprexa Zydis to treat his psychosis but without resolution. He remained disorganized and psychotic, and it was felt prudent to transfer to API for further assessment and stabilization. The patient was cooperative with escort to the interview room. He was malodorous and appeared disheveled. The patient spontaneously offered several bizarre tangential narratives with delusional content. He referenced having his voice stolen by an Alaskan Native, and therefore, he must talk in an accent. He then assumed a British-style accent but stated he was actually from Germany. He referenced "moral clouds" and how he interacts with them. He displayed loose associations, and overall, he was quite disorganized. He had difficulty answering basic interviewing questions; for example, when I asked if he has seen a doctor recently, he responded with an explanation of how he doesn't like doctors, but he likes docks in the ocean and that he is actually a sailor; and overall, it was difficult to elicit reliable information. He self-identified as feeling in psychiatric crisis. He states he comes to API periodically for a "check-up." He denies feeling suicidal or homicidal.

MENTAL STATUS EXAMINATION: He appears thin. He makes sparse eye contact. His affect is mildly anxious. There was no display of agitation. He was cooperative, pleasant, and easily engaged. His speech was rambling. He was alert and fully oriented to person, place, date, and situation. His memory and concentration are distracted. Judgment and insight are impaired.

This was when my sisters and I learned of the boat, of Tom's camp across the street. Dad hadn't mentioned it to us. I didn't ask why. It was easy enough to guess. Probably it was just too painful—too difficult to say out loud, three times, to three different daughters.

But now, suddenly, Tom was saying yes to the help he was offered—including medication. He stayed at API for a few months, during which time his treatment went beyond merely minimizing symptoms to include "person-centered" therapy, which would help him learn how to manage his illness and build the skills he would need to function consistently in day-to-day life. Eventually he signed a release-of-information form, allowing API to contact Dad, who visited and noted that Tom was beginning to seem a bit like his old self again. I began to believe that this thing had finally turned around, that Dad's terrible gamble was at last paying off.

But in August, after Tom was transferred to a halfway house, he had trouble there and was sent back to API for another stint. And sometime around then, unexpectedly, he revoked the release of information and cut off all communication with Dad. He didn't say why he did it, but I suspect it had to do with finding himself again without an adequate place to live—that this brought up his old anger at Dad or triggered his paranoia. Whatever the case, it meant that Tom would be attempting the difficult process of rebuilding his life on his own, without Dad's help.

And he faltered. His second stay at the halfway house did

of the episode, he had left. Whether this was by his choice or theirs, she couldn't tell.

The episodes had happened, too, at API, where they had been bad enough that the staff had physically restrained him at least once. This was scary for him, had grown warped in his memory, and he spoke sometimes of API as a bad place. But he was also confused about that, telling Adrienne that he thought perhaps API staff had not actually restrained him but had instead sent him to jail. It came out that he hated jail, that it was a hard, harrowing place for him. He said repeatedly that it frightened him. That was the word he used—*frightened*. What was worse, he didn't seem to know what he had, in the past, been arrested for. It was as if jail was something he couldn't see coming, something he felt could just happen to him without warning. So, he explained, he had decided that if he ended up in jail again, he was just going to close his eyes. That was how he would manage. He would just keep his eyes closed.

Now he was worried about API as well, because if API had sent him to jail, that meant he could never go back to API either. Adrienne, listening to it all, was struck by the depth of his confusion, and by the genuine need with which he asked her what she thought had happened. "He had a sense that he didn't know," she told me, "but didn't know what part he knew and what part he didn't." When she checked with API about their policies and reported back to him that API would not have sent him to jail for any reason, Tom was immensely relieved. So she pressed the point that API was a safe place, and kept talking about it, trying to assure him that he could always return there.

There was a voice, too, that frightened him. A bad voice, a voice that he could hear coming back now that he was off his medication. It was talking to him while he spoke to Adrienne, telling him things about her, things that were not good, though he refused to say what. He knew, he said, that it was just a voice. A nurse at API had talked about it with him, teaching him how to deal with the voice, how to question it, how to choose to ignore it. And for a while, medication had made it disappear. Adrienne called API and tried to speak with that nurse, but he would not return her calls. We figured that he was probably not allowed to speak to her without Tom having signed a release of information.

Even while homeless, Tom was still trying to apply the skills he had developed at API. He had learned the importance of having a routine, and he kept a daily schedule that he carefully followed, walking each day after lunch to the public library. It seemed that the care he received at API had truly helped him, and just as much that he wanted to keep helping himself. Not understanding why he had abandoned his treatment, Adrienne asked if he disliked his medication. But he said no, he didn't mind it. Why, then, did he stop taking it? "Because," he said, "I don't think that's what God wants for me."

It was comically, cosmically sad.

I was impressed by what Adrienne had accomplished. She had done everything right, everything I felt I could not have managed if I had been in her place. "I would have collapsed," I told her.

"I did," she said. She caught the flu, and when she got back to Santa Fe, still sick, she went out and got drunk with some friends—loud and rowdy and jubilant, standing on a table, taking off her shirt—until it got late and the bartender cut them off and she felt herself flip into a kind of post-traumatic shutdown in which she couldn't speak, couldn't be around people. And a guy she was with thought she was being rude and turned on her, angry, accusatory. She ran out onto the back stairs and called her ex-boyfriend and asked him to talk her down because he was the only person who knew how. And he did. And then she went back into the bar but her friends had all gone home.

I had assumed that when Tom sought help of his own accord, the mental health system would be there to provide what he needed, with or without Dad. I was now beginning to see how dramatically wrong I had been. The whole tactic of pushing him into homelessness now felt deeply, painfully misguided. It had taken four years for it to drive him to seek help—four years of isolation, trauma, and unremitting psychosis—and now his homelessness seemed to only be keeping him ill.

I ran my mind in circles trying to come up with new ideas. I was by now researching schizophrenia in earnest, for my own writing, but most of what I learned was not directly applicable to solving our problem. And as before, my thoughts were not new to Dad. The only viable long-term solution to Tom's problems appeared to be what social services referred to as "permanent supportive housing"—an apartment where he could not only live but also get the extra assistance he would need to live safely and comfortably over the long term. Staying at one of Anchorage's halfway houses, where he could get help and guidance with daily living and medication, was supposedly a necessary step toward reaching the next level of independence, but these transitional residences didn't appear to have the quiet and private space that Tom needed.

If it had been up to me, I might have tried some of my other ideas just to see if they could work. But it was not up to me, and to be fair, I had not devoted the time to the problem that Dad had. "I have spent hundreds of hours thinking about this," he sometimes told me, "maybe thousands." In one frustrated email exchange, he wrote, "It is not like these ideas never occurred to me. I have been working on this since Panama and have not found a solution. I would love it if someone would show me the way."

The fact was, this had gotten away from us. And Tom was a moving target. For a long time, his words about God were as baffling to me as anything he had ever said. Only much later did they start to make sense, as it dawned on me how hard he had been trying to help himself when Adrienne saw him, as I grasped that he couldn't manage the system's demands. It occurred to me that, if he had wanted to keep taking his medication, his inability to tolerate the halfway house environment would have cost him his access to it. I began to suspect that his idea about God was not a cause but a justification—that, unable to get his hands on his medication after leaving the halfway house, he concluded that it was not what God intended.

Tom was trapped in what activists in mental health circles often spoke of as the "revolving door" of care that people living with schizophrenia are commonly subjected to in this country—round after round of crisis care with little or no follow-up. This leads to patients deteriorating again, maybe getting picked up by police again, being delivered back to jail or the hospital, only to be released into circumstances in which they deteriorate again. There are many ways it can go, but the results are the same.

As one more winter descended with Tom outdoors, I asked Dad if he would consider letting Tom live with him once more. He sighed and said, as he often had, that he felt strongly that it was wrong to enable him to avoid treatment. He wanted to keep pushing Tom to accept the housing that was available. But he also said that at some point, he had realized he needed to start taking care of himself as well as Tom. The last several years had been so taxing, endlessly and unremittingly, that he wasn't sure he had it in him to care for Tom at home again, even if he had thought it was a good idea.

So we kept searching for new approaches. Some seemed promising. I had begun seeing articles about larger cities that were experimenting with Housing First programs, which focused on housing the most vulnerable, difficult-to-help, chronically homeless people by giving them apartments with no strings attached. Traditional approaches required first completing other steps like engaging in treatment for mental illness or addiction. This new approach, which was proving to be surprisingly successful, would not have required Tom to acknowledge his schizophrenia or navigate a complicated system or even take medication in order to receive care and a permanent residence, but would have provided him with a home first, and then consistent support and encouragement in dealing with his illness—ideally as much as he needed. In Anchorage, a Housing First program had recently been launched for people with addiction problems, but implementation for those with mental illness was still years away.

I returned home again in the summer of 2012, hoping I could help turn things around. At the very least, I could gather information about how Tom was getting by. Maybe what I found could give us a sense of how to go forward from there.

Will came with me, his first trip to Alaska, and I wanted to take him to Girdwood and other favorite places, but I warned him that I wouldn't leave town until I found Tom, and maybe not at all, depending on how things went with him. We spent the first day driving around, searching—up and down Northern Lights, up and down Fourth and Fifth Avenues. On the second day we went for a long walk on the Coastal Trail, partly so I could show it to Will but mostly to look for Tom. Dad suggested checking the two soup kitchens and the Brother Francis Shelter, where Tom stayed regularly when he wanted to sleep indoors. The first place we tried was closed, but the employees who were cleaning up recognized my description of Tom and said he was there often. Then we went a few blocks over to the shelter, where I asked about Tom at the front desk. "A white gentleman?" the woman asked. "Red beard?" Yes, yes. "Keeps to himself?" Yes.

She knew Tom but wasn't allowed to say if he was staying there, so she said I could leave a note on the bulletin board in the front vestibule. She also suggested that in the morning I try Bean's Cafe, the soup kitchen next door. I tore a scrap of paper from my notebook and wrote down my phone number along with a few words to Tom. As I tacked it to the board, I glanced at the other messages that had been left. I had never thought about other people going looking for their homeless relatives—others like me, the ones with homes who knew and loved someone without. I felt silly for having never thought of that, and sillier still to be leaving my message. I was sure Tom wouldn't call me. And though I told myself that at least he'd know I was looking, I realized he probably wouldn't notice my note at all.

I had somehow never felt so silly in my whole life. My helplessness, after so many years, had developed an edge that I kept cutting myself on. Our intractable failure sprang back on me, turning my love for my brother into a farce, making my every effort on his behalf appear stupid and moot. To be asking around for him like that—the whole exercise of it was absurd, incomprehensible even as it happened. Even as I walked next door to the café, as I asked the servers if they knew him, as a man told me yes, Tom had been eating breakfast there lately. Even as, the next morning, I walked again into the soup kitchen and found him standing at a bookshelf right by the entrance, scanning a paperback.

"Tom," I said, the word like a rock in my mouth.

"Oh hey, Marin," he replied, then held up a finger. "Hang on a sec. I need to finish reading this." He flipped quickly through the remaining hundred or so pages of the book, not reading so much as glancing at each page rapidly in succession, on toward the end. Will and I stood to the side, waiting awkwardly until he finished. It was clear he was not reading, could not possibly be reading, but his face looked like that of a man who was reading—focused, thoughtful, almost stern with concentration. Will looked baffled. I just watched, wondering what Tom was perceiving.

When he finally set the book down and looked at us, I introduced Will and announced that he was my fiancé. Tom gave him a polite hello, shook his hand, and then turned back to me and ignored Will from that point on. Behind us stretched a long steel countertop lined with people scooping trays of hot foods. As we got in line, I told Tom I had lived in New York for a while and was now a writer. Momentarily intrigued, he began talking about a book he had written in his head. I nodded, feeling almost electric to be standing beside him again, filled with a sense that maybe I was about to fall down.

Tom seemed much the same as before—clean and healthy enough but very skinny. His hair was quite long and tangled awkwardly over his forehead, and his clothes were oddly mismatched—a windbreaker under a rain shell under a sheepskin coat. He was still standoffish and his face was largely expressionless, but his eyes darted to meet mine for brief moments, revealing again the unshielded quality I had seen before. He asked no questions, didn't wonder what I was doing in

Anchorage or how long I would stay. But he kept talking to me. And as he spoke he leaned in, getting close so I could hear him over the din, gesturing with one hand as we sat at a long cafeteria table in the big square room.

The conversation went on for nearly an hour, his usual pre-occupations, as Will looked quietly around and I absorbed what I could. I asked all the questions—where do you sleep, what do you eat, do you need a hat, gloves, pants. But I got only obvious answers or no answers. I told him the family's news: Adrienne was pregnant and would have a baby in a month or so, which surprised and cheered him. But I was a bit dazed just to be with him, and all I could think to say was what I had already decided to say. Tom, come by Dad's house. Tom, here is some cash. Tom, I love you. Tom, I've missed you. Tom.

Then, without preamble, he said, "The world looks at me, and sees a bum." He shot me a glance, gauging my reaction. I stared, a little amazed that he knew what the world thought of him—wishing suddenly that he didn't have to know it—and more amazed that he would acknowledge it to me. He con-tinued, "But I know that I am not a bum. I am a saint. I am close to God." With that, he closed his eyes and softly lifted his chin, as if retreating into a space where none of this mattered.

Eventually he began to seem uncomfortable—more dis-tracted, more nervous. I wondered if his voices had started up, or maybe had been there all along and now had worsened. He paused periodically and waited as if listening to something. "This is enough now," he said.

"Can I come back tomorrow?" I asked. He thought a moment.

"I don't know," he said, looking at me sternly. He stood, picking up his empty food tray. I watched his face, the form of it. The square jaw, the wide bone of his nose, the brow ridge pulling inward in thought and maybe fear. How much more often had I expected to see that face in my life? How many more glances had I expected from those eyes, comments from that mouth? I kept recalling the time he admonished me, "Marin, stop being so hard on yourself." I couldn't even remember why he had said it or what we were doing. Just the way it came out, equally exasperated and encouraging. How much more of that, exactly—whatever that was? And how badly did I want him to tell me, right then, to stop being so hard on myself?

"We don't have to talk long if you don't want to," I said.

"I don't know."

The next day I showed up alone, soon regretting it, feeling Will's absence acutely. I still could not believe that this was our life—stepping across the parking lot to the cafeteria, past the clusters of men who idly watched me as I searched for the one among all of them who was mine. I had never felt so exposed, so raw. It all struck hard and mowed me down.

I walked in and soon found Tom. But something had solidified overnight. He didn't want to talk to me. Too quickly he was turning away, and I was asking why, trying to stall. He paused and said, "I can't forgive you."

"For what?" I asked, sinking inside. Again, he focused inward and then gave me a suspicious look.

"For your crimes." His face was a wall.

I didn't ask what crimes, just said a few more things, trying to soften the moment, hoping to wriggle past the rejection, though I could see in his eyes that there would be no appeasing him. Abruptly, he turned away and got in line for food. I stood in my spot, unable to move, staring at the back of his head for what seemed like a long time. Finally I noticed people looking at me and I turned to go. That was the last time I ever saw him.

There Is the Urge to Find Meaning

THERE WAS THE DREAM ABOUT THE RAVEN. I CLIMBED alone into a box canyon to find it there, sitting on a boulder among several small, mossy pools. Behind it, stones piled up to create a wall blocking off the back of the canyon. Geometric sandstone cliffs rose above us, vertical and marked with innumerable cracks and crevices. We were in our own room, still and quiet and separate.

The bird sat askew, one wing lopsided, falling forward slightly and hanging low. Broken. It looked at me and did not move.

I worked my way toward it and still it didn't move, only cawed at intervals. So I stepped through a stream to the far side of the boulder and climbed up. It hopped lightly as I sat down beside it, but it stayed. We looked at each other, two feet apart. I was so close I could see the bright yellow skin that rimmed its eyes.

There was the fact that it was not a dream. Only seemed like one. Seemed far removed from the ordinary fun of our camping trip—of friends and Will and his kids and the Colorado River tributary we had played in all day.

A pale bone was visible at the joint of the wing, and a touch of red that once had been blood. "How did you break your wing?" I asked, thinking. The bird's head cocked one way, then the other. It cawed. Its eyes, as it peered at me, were a bluish slate gray. It examined me as if I were a mystery.

Then I saw that its bill curved sharply at the tip, to the left. It was misshapen, a soft bend, not unlovely. "Oh," I said aloud, "deformed." It cocked its head again. I felt alarmed. What was happening here? It was then that I saw its gape: At the rear corners of its bill were two small, bright yellow flaps of skin. "But you're a baby!" I said. Barely a fledgling.

The bird cawed. I gazed at it a long moment. The broken wing, the gape, the fearlessness, the inquisitive eyes. The misshapen bill. I added it up. "You fell out of your nest," I said. And the tears just fell out of me. I let them flow down my cheeks without wiping them away.

My brother was in jail that day, and I was glad. It meant he was warm, and fed, and likely taking medication. He had been arrested a week before for aggressively reacting to a woman who, seeing him walking in traffic, had pulled up and admonished him to get out of the roadway. He had lashed out at her, elbowed her in the forehead, gotten charged with misdemeanor assault. I was grateful to her. It must have been apparent that he was homeless. I had almost cried when I learned she wasn't hurt. And then I wondered what she thought of him.

The day before, at the campground, I had watched four young men in the site beside ours. I happened to glance over as one skillfully walked a slackline strung between two trees. I took in the shaggy brown hair, the lean bare torso, the long shorts. My face crumpled just as Will walked up, saw the boy, looked back at me, and said, "Your brother?"

"He looks so much like him from behind."

.

I wandered back into a box canyon, alone, and found a raven, beautiful and dying. This bird was born, had a mother, lived briefly in a red rock enclave deep in Arizona's Havasupai reservation, and met me before meeting its end.

We sat there for long minutes as I talked my way through the clues, putting the pieces together. The bird cawed occasionally, cocked its head, its eyes so open, so wide—wide on the inside, absorbing everything.

"You're going to die, aren't you?" I said. I looked up into the high cliffs, searching for the ledge with the nest from which he must have fallen, wondering how many days this bird had had on this earth. How many more there would be. I couldn't save him, I knew. We had hiked a long way in.

A life only a few weeks long—an intelligent, emotional life—spent entirely within this canyon room. The low boulders on which his droppings hung, signs that he could hop about. The crystal stream trickling through crystal pools. The brilliant green moss, the water ferns. The shape of the sandstone. A decent life, it seemed, however short.

I tried to feed the bird some salami. He darted for it and I watched him fumble with it in his malformed bill, awkwardly trying to toss it back down his throat before accidentally dropping it into a still pool. We peered down over the edge of the rock, together, at the sunken salami. Then as we stared at each other, he looked back at me as if abashed and I registered the depth of his ignorance. I felt the *oops* hanging between us, and he seemed to ask, *But can you give me some more?*

I gave him some more. He couldn't even eat without messing up.

.

It was nearly a year since I had seen Tom last, one of only a handful of times in a long decade. So often in places, in circumstances, I could barely imagine. Soon he would agree to let his assault case go through the mental health court, and would accept treatment as part of his sentence. The court would order him to make an appointment at the local community mental health center and work with staff there to develop a plan of care. A probation officer would be assigned to him to monitor his progress. But as long as he was rejecting Dad's help, the onus was entirely on him to make it happen. He would have to keep track of the phone number, remember to call, figure out where to go, catch a bus or two, and show up on time—all on his own, all without a daily dose of his antipsychotic. And that was just for the first appointment. It would take many to achieve anything lasting. This is what was required of a homeless man with severe, chronic, untreated schizophrenia. It was virtually impossible.

There is the urge to find meaning. Maybe dreams always mean something. They are fictions. In them every image can be taken as a cipher, with every strange scenario hiding the useful metaphor, the one that rings true, revealing the problem that has secretly preoccupied you and is maybe the reason you remembered the dream. But in life, things are what they are. First and foremost, perhaps only and entirely. This bird was not a metaphor. He was alive. And yet it is odd: how perfect the setting, the series of events. I felt that the bird had a message for me, but although I tried I could not read it.

What did I appear to be, in the mind of this bird? Ravens, I knew, are ingenious problem solvers. They have language too—some forty calls with which they speak to one another.

They form attachments, strong bonds, just as we do. Perhaps they share the same symbolic consciousness—the capacity for thought, inseparable from language—that we feel to be so human. Perhaps they, too, can find meaning in things.

I, a being that appeared out of nowhere, sat beside him, spoke to him, gave him food, and then departed, returning to the unreachable place from which I had come. Was I an emissary from another world? Did I seem, to the bird, to have a message? Were we one another's envoy?

After I left our boulder to explore the canyon, I saw the mother. She flew overhead, and I turned back to see the young bird hopping from stone to stone, attempting to follow her as she passed over, cawing a loud, scratchy *crack*. She returned the call from high above, the same harsh note from her sleek silhouette, but she did not stop.

The next day Will climbed up into the canyon and found the bird dead. I had refused to join him, not wanting to see. He took a long tail feather and gave it to me for remembrance.

I once heard Leslie Silko say that sometimes, ceremony is the only resolution we can have.

Later I plunged from the top of a waterfall. There was a moment when I hung in the air, having jumped but not yet falling. The world was all blue and the water so very far beneath me. *This jump*, I told myself, *is for my baby bird*. I shut down my fear.

Down in the deep pool, the world was again all blue. I descended slowly, my body a V. I hung in the water.

Vagabond

DID I KNOW, THEN, THAT WE WOULD LOSE? TEN YEARS HAD passed since I first suspected Tom had schizophrenia, and it was only taking a greater toll. Months later, as Christmas neared, Dad saw him walking and stopped the car. Tom looked ragged and Dad asked him several times to come by the house, suggesting he get some good winter clothes, but Tom declined and soon politely turned to go. "I am definitely a persona non grata these days," Dad noted. So it continued. A few months later, when Dad spotted him again, Tom waved but changed directions and kept walking. Dad was at a loss. "I don't know which is more difficult," he wrote, "seeing him or not seeing him."

It was a sign of Dad's bewilderment that one day, unexpectedly, he wrote and asked me for advice: "Has all of your study given you any new ideas regarding Tom?" I sat for a few moments before responding, trying to conjure some better answer than the one I had to give: No, it had not. It almost stung, the question, forcing me to acknowledge what I had preferred to deny. There was something painful, too, in Dad's phrasing. *All of your study.* The grasping, the sense of totality. *All the king's horses, all the king's men.*

In February, something finally gave way. The Brother Francis Shelter changed an important rule about when and for how long a person could sleep on one of its cots. It had been the shelter's policy that after sleeping there for thirty nights straight, you had to spend one night away before returning for up to thirty more consecutive nights. Then, in the deepest part of winter, the policy changed: Now a person had to spend a full thirty nights away before returning for another month. And that year, as was typical, a mid-February cold snap brought temperatures down to single digits for several days. Suddenly stuck out in the cold, Tom overstayed his welcome somewhere and was asked to leave. When he refused, the cops came and arrested him for trespassing. It was Valentine's Day—a day I celebrated that year with Will at an expensive French restaurant. Tom spent it back in jail.

For the next month he was held in the correctional facility's mental health unit and was, records say, very fearful of everyone. His symptoms were as bad as they had ever been— "chronic responding to internal stimuli, both auditory and visual hallucinations, pacing, and some symptoms of mania, including not sleeping for periods up to 24 hours." His physical condition had deteriorated as well, and he had a rash caused by either scabies or bedbugs.

To be rendered competent for his coming court appearances, he was given risperidone, but he kept cheeking the pills, so the doctors had to switch him to a liquid form. By mid-March, the antipsychotic was having its effect. He was for the first time making eye contact, and in general was far less afraid of others—though he could still be, the doctor noted, "quite fearful if challenged." He was still hallucinating too, and when he spoke, in a low stream of rapid and unceasing speech, he seemed genuinely unable to stop midsentence to answer questions. Deemed still not competent to stand trial, he was transferred to API for his third and final stay there.

The exchanges in Tom's last intake interview, when I read them now, feel at once bizarre and familiar, funny and sad—full of images that, depending on my mood, strike me as either profound or absurd. When asked if he had ever had a head injury, Tom said, "I've been hit in the head more than anyone who's ever been."

FORENSIC ADMIT EVALUATION
Admission Date: Mar 14, 2014

MENTAL STATUS EXAMINATION: The patient is unable to state why he is being admitted to API. He announced that he believes himself to have Downs' Syndrome and referenced this condition several times during the admission interview. However, he clearly presented as far more intelligent than this condition would predict. Much of what he said was inaudible and, when understandable, was often nonsensical. He was clearly responding to auditory and visual hallucinations and reported that the "spirit" of the [psychiatric nursing assistant] was alternately sitting and standing next to the PNA. He seemed to be carrying on conversations with other beings in the room at times, possibly checking in with them before answering questions. He had difficulty providing personal history or focusing his attention for any length of time. His judgment and insight are poor. His memory appeared to be negatively impacted by his active psychosis. It was not possible to directly measure his general fund of knowledge. He does not exhibit understanding of his legal status.

By the time Tom contacted Dad, that May, his condition had improved significantly. He was taking lorazepam for anxiety, melatonin for insomnia, and risperidone for psychosis, as well as benztropine, which reduces agitation. His previous diagnosis of undifferentiated schizophrenia had been called into question by his manic symptoms, and now the report included notes on his manic state and the need to rule out "bipolar disorder with psychotic features." Dad began visiting Tom regularly in API's locked ward and, at some point, was told that Tom had been diagnosed with schizoaffective disorder— the same illness I had long suspected Mom had.

Tom clearly didn't want to spend another winter outside, but he believed his only solution was to go to prison. He said he was preparing himself for that eventuality, as it seemed unavoidable. Dad countered by explaining that if he cooperated with the system that existed to help him, he would never have to go back to jail. Tom was slated to leave API in mid-June, at which time he would have his court hearing and would likely be released for time served. His treatment team seemed to be doing their best for him, hustling to find him transitional housing, and we heard that they liked him, found him kind and polite. But with the chronic shortage of both staff and beds at API, they needed to get him out of their care as quickly and efficiently as possible. So Dad focused on talking to him about what would come next, speaking positively, being optimistic, trying to empower Tom to work with the people who could help him.

It wasn't clear if the message was sinking in, but Dad stayed at it. Wanting to remind Tom of how much awaited him if he got well, he brought photos of my sisters and their children, and of my wedding day. He also asked me if he could tell Tom about my depressions, and asked Adrienne if he could share that she had for a while taken the mood stabilizer lamotrigine, thinking this would help him feel less alone. Tom was surprised to know that we had had our own struggles with mental health, and I hoped he found it encouraging.

In June, Tom gave permission for us to call him. It had been at least seven years since we had last talked on the phone, and two since we last stood face-to-face. It felt surreal to simply dial a number from my house in Tucson and ask for him. So bafflingly easy. And just as baffling, just as easy, was the way he said in his gentle voice that he loved me, he missed me, he was glad to talk to me. It was clear right away that he was far, far more coherent than when I had seen him last. But I could also feel the schizophrenia still in his speech, tightening and stilting his thoughts. His sentences, short and direct, phrases repeated too often, the wording always identical. *Flattened. Stereotyped.* Words in toneless bursts. Long pauses after I spoke, as if he struggled to process my statements.

I called him four times in as many weeks, each call building on the last, but each one also strangely redundant. Thinking about his circumstances, trying to sort out how to move forward, he told me more about his life in that one month than in the entire previous decade. But his mind was still muddled. When I asked him questions, trying to draw out his concerns so that I could address them, it was hard to tell how much of it was landing. And although he seemed to quite like API, saying it was nice and that the people there were helpful, it was clear that his trust—in us, in the system, in everything—was tenuous. On our first call he announced, in a heavy tone, that he wanted me to know that after he left API he believed he was going to have to end up in jail. When I assured him that this could be avoided, and that everyone was going to do their best to make sure it would be, he said simply, "Thank you for saying that." And though it was a kind reply, it flustered me. I didn't quite know how to read it—if it meant he believed me and felt better, or if it was a way to say he appreciated my concern but didn't think it would amount to much.

He told me he was reading *The Great Gatsby*. Surprised, I asked how much of it he had read. I felt hopeful, but unsure whether this meant he was reading or just that he thought he was reading. "The first couple of chapters," he answered. "It's pretty good."

"What do you like about it?" I asked.

"I like the scenes with the people just sitting around enjoying each other's company," he said. "Drinking beverages and talking to each other. And there's one part where they all go for a ride in a car."

Suddenly sad, I said, "That sounds really pleasant."

"It would be nice to do things like that," he continued. "It kind of reminds me of our grandfather." To my mind's eye came Grandpa in his vintage convertible Cadillac—pale cream, with brown leather seats and round, smooth fifties curves. He sat wearing his white Stetson, one hand on the wheel, the other beckoning us all to hop in for a ride down the narrow ranch roads to the creek. I could see Tom, nine years old, sitting on the seat back, perched high as we passed through the orchards and fields. Tom had wanted to be like Grandpa. I remembered him standing by the creek in the too-big, weather-softened Stetson Grandpa gave him. His old eagerness, his wide grin.

I had a feeling that Tom understood, as I did, that even if he did everything he could to get well, nothing was ever going to bring him all the way back to his former self. Then I was thinking, with a shock, what a luxury it is to sit with a drink among friends, to go for a ride in a car. I was thinking about the characters in *Gatsby*—their ease, their wit, their grace. "You can do that," I said, forcing myself. "You can have all those things."

"I don't know," he said. "I don't know if I can."

"Sure you can," I insisted. "Why can't you?"

He paused. "I don't know if I can support myself—if I'll be able to support myself." A little bit stunned, by both his fear and his honesty, I asked if anything else was worrying him. He said, "I don't know what's going to happen to me when Dad dies."

It was almost with a sense of being outside myself that I replied, "You have Adrienne and me, and Alicia, and we'll always make sure you get what you need after Dad is gone."

Again came his refrain: "Thank you for saying that."

I have been haunted by Tom's final weeks—what I did and didn't do, what was said and not said. Adrienne and I both thought of flying home, but it was a bad time. She had a new-born and I was about to fly to New York to teach a four-week class. Tom asked Dad if he could move back in with him, but Dad said he didn't think it was a good idea. Instead he promised to help him apply for housing. I winced when I heard this, but said nothing.

We were bolstered, however, when he was deemed competent to attend his hearing and when, afterward, his release date was pushed back to late July, giving him more time to improve before having to take the next step. To help prepare him mentally, Dad brought him a new pair of boots and they talked about what clothes to bring for his release. They talked about Tom visiting the house again. They played checkers in a game that dragged on and on until they had to call it a draw. "I can tell you whatever part of Tom's brain deals with checkers is still in great shape," Dad wrote. "I was doing my best to beat him." He added, "I am not sure how all of this is happening???" For a moment, I allowed myself to feel elated.

I tried to discern progress week by week, but I could not. Each time I called Tom, I asked if he would like me to call again. He always said yes, so I promised I would. Yet when I did, he sounded surprised, as if he either had forgotten the previous week's promise or hadn't believed it. He did, however, seem on track to succeed after his discharge from API. He told me outright that he had been diagnosed with schizophrenia—a stunning admission—although he believed it was a mistake. He had decided to just let the doctors say he had schizophrenia since that was necessary to qualify for housing and disability benefits. Confused, I asked how he felt about his medications. And to my relief he said that they made him feel better and the side effects did not bother him, so he was content to keep taking them.

It seemed that we had finally arrived somewhere. He would not need to believe he had schizophrenia so long as doctors and social workers kept working around it as they apparently had been. I saw then how this could work out for him.

But his fear for his future was deeper than I realized. It plagued him. And it was still so strange to me that he feared for his future at all that I never registered the fear's sudden extremity. He was determined not to return to the street, and most days he was stuck sitting around without much to do besides stew in his worries, as API lacked the resources to provide many therapeutic activities. I learned later that as his release date approached, he kept checking in with his case manager, popping into her office every day, asking if she was sure that his housing application would go through, wondering if she had gotten a reply yet. Each day she told him not to worry, half calming him and half brushing him off.

In subsequent calls, I asked again what worried him, hoping to help him feel more confident. He replied with more questions, specific enough that it was clear he had been mulling things over. What if he ran out of medication while living at the halfway house? And he couldn't get more? What if the pharmacy was too far to walk to? What if the pharmacy was closed? Would they kick him out of the halfway house? This made sense of his belief that going to jail was the only solution: It was the only form of housing he could envision working out for him.

I tried to sound assured, always, telling Tom he could ask Dad for help, saying we would have a plan to deal with those issues. He would press on, unsatisfied, considering every potential problem, believing each one could undo him. Not knowing what else to say, I told him I would personally help him deal with whatever came up. At the end, always, came his cryptic reply. "Thank you for saying that."

Five days later, he failed to turn up at lunch. No one noticed—he must have known they wouldn't—until the meal was over, and when staff went looking for him, they found that he had locked himself in a bathroom. Inside he lay dead.

Slide

I REMEMBER WINTER AS IT ONCE WAS, IN CHILDHOOD—absent of terror, no sort of metaphor, only beautiful and nothing more. Alyeska, our mountain, the flanks on which we learned to ski. Days when clouds banked the terrain so thick that the sky and slopes fused, erasing contours so you had only the flex in your knees and your amber goggles to know the shape of the land. Charging through dense snow, skis pulled at by heavy chunks, eating shit as often as not. On easy runs, pointing downhill and going straight to the bottom in as few turns as possible. The ecstasy of speed.

Bodily memories overwhelm me sometimes: lying in Dad's cabin in early-morning darkness, awakened by the sound of bombs on Alyeska while the town of Girdwood slept beneath it. I would listen to the muffled *boom, boom,* easing out of sleep and letting the distant noise lull me, knowing it meant there had been a dump of overnight snow, that the runs were thick with powder and ski patrol was bringing down avalanches, making the mountain safe for skiing. Sometimes I would reach up and pull back the curtain from the small window above the big loft bed, a sister or friend asleep beside me, and look to see if the sky was clear. And in the half sleep that followed I could already feel the mountain beneath my skis. My edges cutting the heavy coastal snow. My body floating up and sinking through the turns.

The dangers of nature are something Alaskan teenagers survive first and understand later. I was home on winter break from college one year when the bombs failed us. A high cornice between Alyeska and adjacent Max's Mountain broke off and released a slide onto Max's while the main part of the ski area, on Alyeska, was open. I stood watching from the cafeteria, a wide building at the base with a wall of windows facing the slopes where the two mountains joined. I paused, holding my chili, and stood agape as half of Max's Mountain came away. A white sheet, unzipped and falling. For a moment I wondered if all those tons of snow would slide right into the cafeteria. If I should run. And then it was easy to gauge that running would do no good.

Luckily the slopes of Max's—outer areas not regularly used—were closed to skiers at the time. Nobody was hurt. But I watched as the slide carried a bright yellow snowcat down into the creek gorge. The cat was parked on a track halfway up the mountain when the avalanche plucked it up and rolled it until it came to a halt, half buried, nearly at the bottom. I thought of those children's construction toys, picked up like nothing by small careless fingers.

A few years later I got a job as a lift operator, checking tickets and helping skiers onto the chairs and shoveling snow off the platforms. One day the Glacier Bowl above Alyeska gave way and a slide crossed into the boundaries of the ski area. Ski patrol evacuated the runs, shut down all the lifts, and gave us long, thin poles, ordering us to probe the mountainside in a disciplined line, searching for buried bodies. Poke, up, step, and on. "Strike!" someone would say, followed by a rush of digging until somebody said, "Rock!" And then we would breathe again and keep going.

Should I continue—on into the sadder memories? Of my friend Johnny, blond and beautiful, who was up in the Alaska Range somewhere near Denali when he rounded a corner and vanished forever. Presumably carried by a small avalanche into a crevasse. Or of that woman Michelle, who died in the backcountry two days after I met her, when above her a young snowboarder let loose a slide that tossed her over a cliff.

A therapist friend, who knew schizophrenia well—she told me, "It is a *miracle* your brother lived as long as he did."

Break My Body

[BARS]

WE BEGIN WITH A BAR AND A LIMB. A BICYCLE HANDLEBAR and an eight-year-old forearm. I fell sideways, put my hand out onto the grassy edge to catch myself. The handlebar found my arm bone, hammered it in two. Next I was fetal, screaming. Tears and heat. My mother carried me through the garage into the house, where she laid me down on a couch and went to call a doctor. "Shock," I heard her say—the doctor's warning. She said it quickly as she stood over me: "She could go into shock." And through the pain I still found a moment, a space in my mind, for curiosity. What was this "shock"? How exactly did she mean that I might enter it?

Another time, and again a bar, a limb. I was a teenage gymnast doing a backflip off a small trampoline. Something went wrong and I flew straight up, flipped, came straight back down. Landed on my shin on the square metal edge of the trampoline. No screaming this time, but the same tears, the same heat. Then I was on my back on the blue-carpeted spring floor, heads circling me—coaches, teammates. I gripped a coach's hand as the muscles in my stomach, my neck, my back seized up from the pain and I fought to breathe, fought to speak. "Adrienne," I croaked. I couldn't relax until my sister's face appeared among the others and I saw her eyes—her look that took in all and gave nothing away. It was enough.

How does the body accumulate its knowledge? Through actions, through injuries. And what I remember best of the most painful physical assaults on my body—the broken arm, the chipped shin—is not myself but the person standing over me. I remember that something was revealed when pain pushed me through the membrane, the invisible psychic boundary, that usually separates each of us from all other things. In that space beyond myself I heard the others, saw them, felt them completely.

Gymnastics celebrates the body but also abuses it. I came home from practices covered in bruises. Small, greenish ones on my hips where I beat against the bar every afternoon. Large multicolored blotches of black, purple, and pink on the outside of my thigh if I fell onto the balance beam. And all types in between, in every imaginable place, most of which I could not remember acquiring and did not recall having suffered for.

It was through gymnastics that I discovered what little girls are made of. We were made of spit and gristle and callused palms, and giggles and neon leotards and fearlessness to a degree that no one over the age of twelve has any right to claim. Our innocence was our power. We could plainly see what we were good for (flight, propulsion) and what we had (muscle, joy). Some in the media worried that veneration of girlhood put us at odds with womanhood. But I don't think that's fair. What put us at odds with womanhood was broader and deeper than sport. It had something to do with the outsize significance others placed on parts of our bodies—breasts, hips, legs— that did not, for us, have the meanings they insisted on.

When I remember gymnastics there are no eyes on me. There is only my body and the objects of my intention. The feel of fine chalk powder on the skin of my palms. The idle habit of rubbing my calluses with my thumb, knowing the hardened skin, its texture, its dimensions. The smell of the leather grips I pulled from their plastic bag; the chalk-dense wristbands drawn over my hands, letting loose clouds of white dust. The grips, each with a strip of suede worn and bent and tugged and wetted and dried to follow the contours of my hand—looping up around the dowel that gave me an extra inch of reach to link my limbs to the bar as I swung, spun, turned, let go, and caught it again. When I wrapped myself around the bar, the chalk rubbed off into the creases of my hips, penetrating the stretchy cotton of my leggings. Back on the mat, I could pull at my leotard and let it snap, releasing puffs of chalk. I breathed it in. The smell, the taste of it against the roof of my mouth: a little bit alkaline, a little bit interesting.

When did that other thing creep in? That shift to seeing yourself through others' eyes. Men's eyes. It comes when they start telling you what they make of you. It comes when you discover that the things they say you are have nothing to do with what you always thought you were. Was it the day my father tugged at my shirt and turned to a friend and said, "Look at that, she's got a waist!" Was it the day on the bus when I overheard two boys behind me sizing me up? "She's a dog," one said. I went home, stared at the mirror, considered my face: *Am I a dog?* Was it when I learned the song we gymnasts sang, about how everyone turned to watch a gymnast girl walking down the street because she had *that strut, that butt*? I couldn't understand why the song unsettled me, so I sang along, about *a million guys* wondering *just how far she'd really go.*

Was this an injury? If not, it was something like one—a betrayal, at least, remaining in the body as betrayals do—stashed in brow muscles that still twitch in recollection. What does it mean that by the time I was sixteen and two boys in my class wanted me to show them my palms because they had heard that my calluses were amazing—their eyes were genuine, impressed—I held back my hands, embarrassed? That I let them look only reluctantly, knowing that my crazy lumps of dense, toughened, yellowed skin were not what the world was going to want me for? Knowing it already too deeply to unknow it, even as my calluses, my badges of honor—of untold hours spent gripping a wooden bar and swinging and banging my body at it, around it, against it—*were* what those boys liked about me in that moment on that day? When did *I* begin to tell *them* what they ought not to like?

[VAULT]

I don't think I understand, really, the strength of women. But I do understand the strength of girls. I understand the teenage Kerri Strug in the '96 Olympics, running and vaulting and landing on a broken ankle after a fall on her first vault broke the bone she then jumped and pounded on. Sticking the landing, winning the medal. I understand the adrenaline charging through her—its power to numb the pain and jack you up so that you trust your limbs and your flips are high. Audiences murmured uncomfortably about her mannish features: the broad-shouldered frame and the chiseled quads that gave her the power to fling her body end over end. They thought she ought to have a different kind of body, the kind of body that could not do what she had just done.

By that time, my own body had lengthened and softened and curved into what America wanted Kerri's to be. My monthly period had finally come a year before, when I was a freshman in college. I tell people this and they say, after a moment of stunned silence, "Oh, because of gymnastics." But I hadn't had a body like an elite gymnast's, like Kerri's—one with so little fat that menstruation dries up, or simply does not come. I was never that strong, that lean. I was thin, but I ate whatever I wanted. Still the periods stayed away for years. In high school, a doctor examined me and assured me nothing was wrong. But I couldn't help feeling like this bloodless state wasn't the right way to be female. It seemed a kind of physical naïveté, a way of not being in on the secret. Then I became that kind of female and it felt like capitulation. I still don't know how to feel about all this. There are so many levels of betrayal at play in the way a woman sees her body that parsing them seems impossible.

Then one day my brother broke his body. It was an irreparable breakage and a final one, accomplished by lodging a wad of paste made from lotion and toilet paper deep in his throat and stopping his own breath. It is not lost on me that the break was achieved not by rending his body asunder but simply by denying it the air it needed to keep moving of its own accord. Denying it agency. He understood that a lack of agency unmakes a body.

But I hadn't known that an assault on another body could break mine too. That grief of this kind is a physical trauma on a massive scale. In grief, my mind's pain became my body's pain and my body's pain reshaped my mind. The pain invaded joints, tissues. The exhaustion was constant. Sometimes I stopped just to pant, winded for no apparent reason. In months two and three I had the sleeping schedule of a small child. Ten, eleven hours a day. Any less and I'd get sick, come down with a cold or a cough. I got two vaginal infections in six months—the same one, recurrent, a yeast-like bacterial bloom that my doctor couldn't explain. For half a year, when people asked how I felt, I said, "Like all my blood vessels have been torn out."

Grief at that intensity shakes you out of the world and out of yourself. In its grip, I shed all my pretenses, not because I wanted to but because I didn't have the energy to resist. I began asking questions of myself that I didn't know were there to ask. I waited all spring to see a childless older friend, just so I could ask for her thoughts about her choice not to have children. I asked without asking: *What should I do?* At a book signing by an author who long ago lost a baby, I told her I'd been unable to write since my brother died. She held my forearm in her hands, hugged me, said kind things as I fought back tears, astounded at myself for breaking down before a stranger. *Who have I become?*

What I'm trying to unravel is the difference between merely existing in a body and truly inhabiting it—to untangle passivity from receptivity. My woman-body has never been as easy for me to love, with its unwieldy breasts and disorienting cycles, as the girl-body that hurled me so beautifully through the air. The woman-body has been good for sex, for attracting Will's touch, but sex is just one aspect of the whole—one that for me has never felt like a primary purpose. And as I find myself choosing not to use the body to create a child, it now seems that the one act its whole design evolved toward will be one it never performs. I'm looking for a new working definition.

[BEAM]

This woman-body is always breaking itself down and building itself back up again. Each month the blood comes out, the mood goes astray, then the system rights itself and continues on.

It's odd how, when the body seems most broken down, some of the most stunning experiences are made. A few months after my brother died, I found myself in a bar at a nineties hip-hop night with a group of friends. Song after song we danced as I rose higher and higher into the rush of music and movement and drink. After midnight I felt euphoria approaching. All at once my skin was electric. I sucked in air and looked up as if through a tunnel of sound, of beats, of swirling lights, of limbs churning and turning. Until suddenly the moment in all its fullness contained only Tom. He was everywhere, everything, in every note and every step. And as he broke over me I felt elation flip into bleak desperation, and I knew that my legs would not hold me and that I would fall. Panicked, I bolted out into the night.

How difficult feeling can be. Like any action, any effort, any cascade of processes the body employs. Breath, heart rate, muscle tension, sweat.

When people used to ask about my bruises from the gym I would shrug and say, "I bruise easily." Girls nodded, said, "Me too." Boys, never.

In her memoir *Conundrum*, Jan Morris, who until midlife had been James Morris, wrote of the intangible difference she felt when she transitioned from a male body to a female one. It was as if her skin were more exposed, she explained, and she could feel the air around her more directly. As if the invisible membrane separating her from all things had evaporated, leaving her nerves more open to her environment. She appreciated this, its vital immediacy, but she also eulogized her days inhabiting a young man's body that was potent and invulnerable and sure within itself. And I thought, *Isn't that what I've always been going for?*

I was alone in New York when I learned that my brother was dead. I had just flown in and was subletting a friend's tiny apartment at 122nd and Broadway when I returned a call from my father and he told me the news. Racked by sudden sobs, as my mind swirled with incomprehension, I felt an agitation come over me and found myself standing, turning, pacing. Needing to escape the confined space, I fled onto the street. For hours I paced the wide avenue, calling friends only to get voicemails, burning with emotion, unable to sit still and unable to reach anyone I knew in the city. I surrendered to the shapes of the other bodies on the sidewalks, to the sound of the cars, the lights undulating through my tears as I roamed up and down Broadway, stopping occasionally to sit on a bench in the median and make another call. It was unlike any experience of being in the city I'd ever had. I was only half aware of it. I was flushed, spastic, wet from constant crying. Tears were lodged in my cleavage, in the creases of my neck, drying into salty crusts in the crooks of my elbows. It was as if all my capillaries had dilated—as if my whole self had dilated, into a pulsing font of tears. Nothing came into focus beyond a few feet away. Instead I felt the city as abstraction, as movement, a flow of footfalls and motors that synced with the pulsing and soothed the panic swelling inside me.

Finally, my friend Sarah got my message. She was in Brooklyn, could reach me in an hour. A few blocks down I turned in through the gates of my old university. It was a mild night and people were milling about as if in a public park. I sat down on the broad steps that led up to the old domed library and waited there.

I say this to tell you that the city rescued me that night. When Sarah saw me sitting high up on the steps she started to run, and took them two at a time, weaving around the pairs and small groups looking out onto the lawns, and as she approached me she held out her arms and I stood and fell into them.

In memory I still see her face above me, somehow nearer and clearer for the pain. And I can still feel the city as it felt then, as intimate a companion as I've ever had. So often in grief I found myself on the edge of both rapture and despair.

[FLOOR]

The following summer I returned to New York and spent several weeks alone there, away from Will. Without his nearness and the soothing of his hands on me, I soon began to feel everything more acutely. At the little zoo in Prospect Park I spent thirty minutes watching the small primates as they climbed over one another, swung, pulled tails, turned upside down to follow the light bouncing off a silver thermos. A marmoset saw me, climbed down a limb toward me. A tamarin peered at me while chewing its food. Their rhythm became my own, and this seemed to say something about us all. The boys, too, break-dancing on the Q train, busking for dollars as it crossed the East River: As they flipped and spun around on the metal handrails, my skin went bumpy and the urge to reach out, to touch them, was so strong that I feared I actually would.

At the end of a long day, my sense of the city would turn visceral. I had moments of near madness on the subway platforms at night. In summer the New York heat is thickest in the train tunnels, and backed by the echoing of voices blending to a murmur and the rumblings of trains flashing by on adjacent tracks, it had the power to undo me. There were times, as a train approached, when the speed jolted me chemically, and grief and cycling hormones pushed me through the invisible membrane without warning, the pain of severance catalyzing some wild connection, and a throb passed through me, a charge flowing out toward the ends of my limbs. I stepped close to the passing train and held out my arms and took in the whipping wind of it, and I felt suddenly glorious with the speed-smoothed steel and the bursts of fluorescent light. And, taking a sharp breath as water filled my eyes, I thought, *This*—

This body's refusal to shield me from sensation, from emotion, from the world. On the contrary, plunging me into them, bashing me against them. This is difficult and it is sometimes incapacitating but it is also something else. I am sure it is a kind of agency. An agency that is about not simply action but also awareness. The claiming of all that a body might know, of what can be gained by not simply withstanding pain but absorbing it, interacting with it, being remade by it.

This is where we land. Feet hitting the floor, body bending and then rising into a last symbolic snap of the arms. Now we must walk off the mat and into the rest of our lives. Into that woman-body and so many other boundless, protean things. Recall that even Kerri Strug was made into something new, something unforeseeable, when she landed the winning vault on that day at the Olympics. Recall that it was barely, barely on two feet that she reached the mat. You could see that she ever so slightly favored the good foot, then put all her weight on it almost immediately as she turned and saluted the judges. That done, she slumped to her knees and bowed her head and paused—the pain hitting hard—and began to scoot off the mat, knees to hands, knees to hands. You could almost feel it with her, in that place where a breakage is also a reaching, almost a joining. Find me there.

That Fragile Space

I WOULD ASK AND ASK AND ASK WHAT LED TOM TO DECIDE to die—what stew of thoughts and visions, what blend of fear and bravery, clarity and confusion, mood and circumstance. I would conclude, for a while, that it was that fragile space between psychosis and sanity that was his undoing—that zone in which he could see all that his life was missing but was still unable to attain it. There is some truth in this, I am sure, though I also felt for a time that fear had killed him. Fear of group housing, fear of the street, fear of jail, fear that we would abandon him. But then sometimes the act seemed surprisingly coherent, intentional. The whole story of Tom's schizophrenia had been a story of demands. All the coping his psychosis required of him, all the compliance the system required of him, all the independence we had required of him. And all the consequences he suffered when he failed or refused. Perhaps in choosing death, he made his death his own.

I briefly suspected his medications, and it's true that lorazepam, a benzodiazepine, can sometimes contribute to suicidality. But eventually that, too, seemed incomplete. The illness itself confers the greatest suicide risk by far. Almost mind-numbingly so—some forty percent of all sufferers attempt it. I would say to myself, *No. Schizophrenia did this. There's no way to parse it further.* Suicide as a complication of mental illness.

I could almost see the death as something that happened outside of storytelling, subject as it was to the nature of delusion. Death as just one moment among innumerable moments, the series achieving form through repetition and juxtaposition, the form more lyric than narrative. The moment of dying standing out only because it would not, could not, be followed by more moments.

This was, it struck me, simply how people die of schizophrenia. It happens by way of suicide or violence or accident, via medication or self-neglect or exposure or some combination of many such things. It happens with the help of stigma and isolation and family dynamics and a horribly flawed system of care. It happens indirectly, slowly or suddenly, often after a long, long slide.

I wonder still what could have been done differently, what would have saved him. Different things at different times, the answer seems to be. The right kind of individual therapy early on, perhaps—someone to help him talk through his experiences and come to terms with them. And later, public programs that Anchorage had not yet implemented. Programs like Housing First and Assertive Community Treatment, through which teams of specialists would track down and assist the severely mentally ill with everything from medication management to grocery shopping. Programs that would enable people like Tom to participate in society rather than push them to its fringes. As it happened, two pilot programs of this kind were launched in Anchorage about a year after Tom died. I read about them in an *Anchorage Daily News* column about an outreach worker who searched through the woods for homeless encampments, seeking those most in need, those who had been on the street for years, to slowly build their trust and convince them to let him help them. I read that often, in the safety and stability of a permanent apartment with regular assistance, participants' symptoms ease up significantly even in the absence of medication. I sat and cried for ten minutes.

My friend the therapist once told me, "There was nothing you could have said or done that would have changed anything." I know she meant it, but I still don't know if I think it is true. And I would like another chance to find out.

Nix

BEFORE THE PANTHEON OF GREEK GODS AND GODDESSES, before even the Titans appeared, there was Chaos. Shapeless and formless, the raw stuff of existence, it was the very first thing to be. Chaos gave birth to many deities, one of whom was Nyx, the embodiment of night. She lived in her palace on the far side of the ocean, at the edge of the cosmos. From her, in turn, sprang Death and Sleep and Dreams—and the Fates, those thread-making sisters who spun and measured and cut the length of every human life, marking its end.

Nyx resided, it was said, in the shadows. She could be seen only in glimpses, from the corner of the eye. You know how, when the night is very dark and nothing is visible when viewed straight on, you have to glance at things sidelong to see them at all.

As a child, I had a phobia of the ocean. Not of water, nor of drowning, nor of any creature in particular. Sharks didn't especially faze me. Yet, walking out into the surf on vacations in Hawaii, I would freeze in terror once my feet could no longer reach the sand. The fear arose because I could neither see my feet nor feel what lay beneath them. They had journeyed to a murky new place where they were vulnerable in their ignorance, and in my ignorance of them.

"Ixnay," declared Robin Williams's Genie in *Aladdin,* "on the wishing for more wishes." *Nix,* in pig Latin. Meaning: no way, not a chance. To nix something is to end it, to cancel it, to condemn it to oblivion. "I can't bring people back from the dead," the Genie also announced, nixing the act of un-nixing. I bring this up because it was one month before Robin Williams killed himself that my brother did the same. Because, like Williams, Tom suffered from a mental illness that had debilitated him for years. But unlike Williams, Tom was poor and solitary and beloved by only a few. Beloved, especially, by me.

I can't tell you what my brother's death meant, but I can tell you that in those first stunned days and weeks after he died, I saw things. That first night, when the news kept me awake and delirious until dawn, I saw my room engulfed by a wave of black ink, which furled across my field of view as if through water until there was nothing to see but its turbulent inky flow. Weeks later, beset by the fact of Tom's end, so bafflingly absolute, I felt as if the wave of ink had hardened into something even more ominous. I told a friend that death now seemed to me like a black wall through which only some could pass. I pictured myself reaching for the wall, straining to peer through it, hurling myself against it. It was horrible in its intransigence. The void was so profound and so present that I knew, for the sake of my sanity, that I had to find a way to imagine something into it.

It is cold at the bottom of the ocean, and largely barren. Once you get beyond the depths to which sunlight can penetrate, photosynthesis is no longer possible. Most of the creatures in the dark zones are hunters or scavengers, living off the remains of what thrives far above—bits of flesh and organic matter that constitute what is called marine snow. These remnants, uneaten by predators, fall gently through the depths, drifting down past the big-eyed predators and transparent invertebrates until stopped by solid ground, which may be miles below. There they feed millions of crabs and urchins and fish of bizarre shapes and features on the vast seafloor. I have seen footage of an army of hagfish, resembling headless eels, skeletonizing a whale carcass before abandoning it to the bone worms.

Tom was not sunken or buried but cremated—rendered molecular and hurled into the atmosphere, leaving only a box of ash to stand in for the body that had once been his. I didn't object to my dad's decision to cremate, but once it happened I panicked. The death itself wasn't even real yet, and then suddenly Tom's whole body was gone too. I kept picturing various parts of him, marveling that they could just blink out of existence. Saying to myself, *Tom's nose no longer exists. Tom's teeth no longer exist. Tom's knuckles no longer exist.* His very bones, immolated. My mind—my intelligence, my sense of self—felt so very feeble in the face of this thoroughly basic, obvious thing.

I don't believe in God, or in any universal creator or divine force, or in an afterlife or anything resembling one. I am an atheist to the core. But I am not a nihilist; I believe that existence is real enough and that meaning is real too. I simply don't think meaning presupposes or preorders existence but rather continually emerges within it, and so remains forever contingent. Maybe this is why I ask myself constantly, endlessly, what things mean. Certainly it is why I'm never satisfied with the answers I find.

How does one engage with nothingness? For months after Tom died I didn't know where to look for him. For a while it was soothing to consider that most of his atoms were floating in the air and that I might breathe him in. That fall, when the nights were just becoming cool at my home in Tucson, I took to wandering out onto the back patio after dark to find myself lying flat on the still-warm bricks, staring upward. The sky was black and vast and clear, largely unaffected by streetlights, with few clouds. Gazing into it calmed me. It resembled a void and yet it was not a void. Things were out there. Between the stars I could envision black holes and distant galaxies and dark matter. The cosmos expanding, and time itself expanding with it. Someday, when all the stars burn out, the universe will go dark.

．　．　．

Some of the moons orbiting Pluto are so small that until recently we did not know they were there. One of these, discovered in 2005, is named after Nyx, the goddess, but was given the alternate spelling of her name: Nix. We knew Nix as no more than a speck until 2015, when it was photographed by the *New Horizons* space probe during its flyby of Pluto. Even then, most of the images of the tiny, oblong moon were so low-resolution that Nix appeared as little more than a pixelated blob. Obscure, indistinct, in the shadow of the god of the underworld.

．

What are we looking for when we look for life on other planets? I thought, had always thought, that we were looking for places similar to Earth. The presence of liquid water with access to sunlight and mineral nutrients—a surface ocean touching rock. No other body in our solar system fits these criteria. They are either blazing hot or frigid. Distant Pluto's terrain runs with liquid nitrogen over a crust of dry ice. On the haze-shrouded surface of Saturn's moon Titan, what flows and evaporates and rains down to shape its stark geography is not water but methane. Ice completely covers Jupiter's Europa and Saturn's Enceladus, but not liquid water. Both are entirely frozen over—skating-rink spheres.

All of the planets in our solar system, with the exception of Earth, are named after Greco-Roman deities. Their moons bear the names of lesser mythological figures. Beautiful Europa was a woman abducted by Zeus, who had taken the form of a bull. Enceladus, which swims amid Saturn's outer ring, was a Giant whose mother, Gaia, desired that he rule over the sea.

Europa has intrigued NASA scientists since 1979, when the *Voyager 2* space probe passed by the small moon on its way past Jupiter. Subsequent Europa flybys in 1996 and 1998, during orbits of Jupiter made by the *Galileo* mission, rendered images clear enough to see that its smooth, frozen surface was extensively scarred by cracks and ridges resembling those on Antarctic ice floes. This suggested that tectonic ice plates were grinding against one another in concert with Jupiter's shifting gravitational pull—that they were being moved about, in other words, by tides. The data revealed also that Europa possessed a magnetic field. This, too, indicated that beneath its surface ice, which is some sixty miles thick, there is water, liquid water—a massive hidden ocean.

My childhood phobia, my sense of an overwhelming lack of knowledge—perhaps I was on to something. Only about five percent of Earth's watery depths have been explored. Visits to the deep sea are so rare that half of today's journeys encounter animals—not just microbes but multicellular organisms—previously unknown to science. All a scientific expedition has to do is go down there and look around, and they're likely to find creatures never seen before by human eyes.

I have often seen my brother in places where he is not. In the eyes or the cheekbones of actors or models, in the shock of hair on a stranger on the street. I have noticed these resemblances ever since Tom first fell ill, and I see them still even though he is gone. They happen, always, by way of a kind of visual cocktail effect in which the likeness leaps out from the corner of my eye to steal my attention before I really know it is happening. He is there, and I turn, and this last part is just the mop-up in which I register why I thought I saw him.

I remember a young man I once knew who fascinated and attracted me. I spent time with him only briefly one summer, and as fall set in I thought of him constantly. After taking a road trip across four states, I drew a series of pictures of him in the landscape through which I had passed. And the thing is, once I had made those drawings I didn't wonder about him anymore. Maybe the looking for him was the real point, or maybe my curiosity simply burned itself out. But it was also as if my act of looking had actually placed him there.

.

I suspect that absence is only ever complete in a literal sense, as received fact. What we make of it, and make with it, and make it into—all of which is real enough—has a way of undoing it. Absence becomes a presence, not nothing but something, almost material, a field of stuff.

. . .

The English word *nix* derives from the German *nichts,* meaning "nothing." The same word, by a different derivation, is also found in Germanic folklore. A nix, those legends hold, is a water sprite—a shape-shifter at home in that wilderness under the waves, dangerous and gifted in disguise.

All life on Earth, I learned in my youth, stems fundamentally from the energy of the sun. Photosynthetic microbes and plants harness sunlight to produce fuel, converting its energy into living matter that other organisms feed on, as they are fed on by others, who are eaten by yet others, and so on across intricate food webs. Without sunlight providing fuel to drive the whole system, I was taught, there would be no life at all.

But this isn't true. At a little over three thousand feet down, the ocean becomes as black as interstellar space. Here begins the midnight zone, the region into which no sunlight penetrates at all. In 1977, the scientist Robert Ballard piloted a submersible deep into the near-freezing gloom of the Galápagos Rift. Eight thousand feet down, on the ocean floor, he found a series of vents spewing magma-heated water from beneath the earth's crust. Some of these hydrothermal vents sent black plumes several stories up into the sea. They consisted of hot brine that, due to the extreme pressure at that depth, did not turn to steam even at temperatures reaching 650 degrees Fahrenheit. The superheated water was loaded, too, with dissolved barium and calcium and hydrogen sulfide, substances considered toxic at high concentrations.

Yet crustaceans and mollusks abounded on the tall, crusty mineral chimneys that grew up around the vents, as did hundreds of tube worms, whose blood-red, gill-like appendages filtered the water. These animals' capacity to survive in such extremes was astounding. But even more so, the entire community was living utterly independent of the sun. Its species relied on neither sunlight nor anything at all from above. The ecosystem's existence hinged on harnessing not the sun's energy but instead the energy released by chemical reactions between minerals dissolved in the hot vent water. This was done through a process called chemosynthesis, performed by bacteria residing within the feathery bodies of the tube worms—a process comparable to photosynthesis, but without light. Those vents, in short, redefined life as we know it.

Discern the nixes at play.

When, in 2004, NASA's *Cassini* spacecraft arrived at Saturn and began exploring its rings, scientists learned that Enceladus's icy surface is striped across its southern polar region with a network of fissures much like those on Europa. As Europa does, Enceladus appears to hold beneath its ice a sizable ocean warmed by gravitational energy. Another flyby revealed that its fissures are coated with colored compounds, and its southern pole is home to a series of enormous jets that shoot sprays of particles hundreds of miles into space. In 2015, after years of data analysis, NASA announced that the particles the moon's geysers blast into Saturn's orbit consist of an icy dust of salts and minerals and simple organic compounds like propane and benzene—nutrient-laden frozen seawater. This means that, unlike anywhere else in this solar system aside from Earth, we know Enceladus to possess all the conditions, both physical and chemical, that are needed for life as we understand it.

. . .

What is under the ice of Enceladus? I can imagine anything into that deep. On some days, I see microbial colonies growing in tall columns on the edge of a continental shelf. Or I envision faintly glowing jelly-bodied creatures, thousands of them linked to form nets. Sometimes I even conjure complex beings—an aqueous civilization—before my imagination collapses under the sheer number of forms life might take.

Consider the oldest known animal on Earth, a deep-sea black coral perched on the flank of an underwater mountain near Hawaii. About a thousand feet down, in what is often called the twilight zone, it lives off marine snow. Radiocarbon dating has shown it to be over four thousand years old.

There are five hundred or so hydrothermal vents that pepper Earth's deep-ocean ridges. It is possible that Enceladus's seafloors possess vents not unlike ours, with chemosynthetic life-forms that function much as ours do. It is possible that Enceladus's life-supporting conditions have been present long enough for life to have evolved there much as it did here—that a "second genesis" has taken place. It is possible, even, that Earth was long ago colonized by microbes that originated on

Enceladus and were hurled into space by its geysers. Or vice versa. Many species of bacteria could survive, dormant, in space for years while a rock carried them from our planet to the rings of Saturn. It is hard to know where to stop with this.

My older sister used to suggest I was intellectualizing mental illness when I spoke of our brother's brain, his schizophrenia, in scientific terms. I didn't think I was doing that, but I never knew how to explain what I felt—that science could be a way of loving something more deeply.

I should tell you, too, that in 1984, a second type of chemo-synthetic ecosystem was discovered on Earth and it, too, lay at the bottom of the sea. Occurring at seafloor seeps—fields of cold sulfurous brine or liquid hydrocarbons that spill from between the continental plates and pool on the ocean floor—these toxic terrains, looking so much like terrestrial marshlands but more closely resembling puddled paint thin-ner, rely on chemosynthetic bacterial mats that harness the fluids' potential energy and provide a primary food source for sprawling colonies of worms and mussels and clams. And I'll tell you that in the months after I learned this, with my head full of facts and memories, I jotted down these words: *I want life to be everywhere.*

Meaning occurs in the spaces between things, doesn't it? From here to Nix it is nearly four billion miles.

I am thinking of metamorphoses, and ancient Greek myths of transformation. Zeus becoming a bull, Daphne turned into a tree, Orion remade as a constellation. When Tom died, I told my mother that it was possible to send off his ashes to a company that would form them, through heat and pressure, into a diamond. "Carbon to carbon," she said ruefully.

In *Europa Report,* a quiet 2013 sci-fi thriller, a team of astronauts travels for more than a year through black space to reach Europa, to explore the possibility that there is life there. The crew lands among the disordered ridges of the Conamara Chaos, a region in which the ice sheet is suspected of containing subsurface lakes. As, one by one, the crew members vanish and the mission collapses, it becomes clear that there is something deadly in the water under the ice. In the final scene, with the landing pod sinking, the solitary pilot, knowing this is the end, decides to die within view of the wall-mounted camera so that it can capture what is coming to kill her. Her last act is to open the air lock and let the water in. As a giant, tentacled, bioluminescent body spirals up toward her through the flooding hatch, she sees the creature. And it is magnificent. Her footage transmits to Earth. Then she is gone.

I am thinking that the truth of my brother's nonexistence, like all great truths, is most difficult to see when I gaze straight at it. Both the absence of Tom and the flashes of him that remain are clearest when I view them sidelong—when twilight gives way to full darkness, after the day's facts have been perused and analyzed and set aside, and I go out alone onto the patio to lie beneath the sky and feel the night engulf me. There, with the bricks at my back, I catch glimpses. About being and nonbeing, existence and absence, cosmos and void. There it is—there *he* is—at the edges of my vision, shadowy and still, as strong and delicate as life itself.

What Remains

1. A BATHROOM, A SOLITARY CUBE OF SPACE. THAT IS WHERE they found him. The rest is questions. Was he on the floor? Did the tiles have a pattern? What color were the walls? Was there a window? Could he see out? What was he wearing? Were his hands cold? Did he feel infinite? Did time seem impossible? What about the future? Was that the worst part? What was the worst part? Was it painful? Did he take a last deep breath? Is that surprising? Should I take a deep breath now, because I can?

2. There are things we wish to say to the dead. I have wished to tell Tom about happiness. I have wished to say that it is not what I once thought it was. That it has lived, paradoxically, in life's interstices, the small gaps that I didn't think meant anything until they accrued. That I could not see it clearly except in retrospect, as a composite formed over time. That it has to do with driving home after school in Dad's Wagoneer with the front bench seat that fit three across—me at the wheel, the radio playing, Tom beside me, Adrienne in a bad mood. And I couldn't tell you what we said or recall any moments espe-

cially, but such moments are what my happiness was made of. They formed the fabric of it and the fabric felt strong and for a long time it was the thing that held me up. And that is how I remember Tom, and it is what I have wanted to say to him about happiness. That there's no trick to it. That it's waiting at the edge of every day, hoping to be noticed.

3. I've been trying to tell you something about Tom. About selfhood and siblinghood and maybe, too, about the places where their boundaries overlap. I want to tell you about the night after his birthday at Y2K. It was New Year's Eve and he had just turned twenty-two, and we were all in Girdwood celebrating at the cabin. We had friends there—Lindsey and Lindsay and a couple of boyfriends and some others—and a few of the girls had snatched some funky polyester clothes from their closets, seventies thrift store finds bought in high school and stuffed away for years, and they now handed them out to all of us because we were partying like it was 1999. I was wearing a turquoise maxi dress covered in purple tropical flowers, and Tom had on some striped bell-bottom pants and a pale blue granny blouse with pastel swirls. That was the night I opened the bottle of Kahlúa I had brought back from Mexico and ruined myself on White Russians for life; the night I slipped comically on the ice as we walked up to the bar at the base of the mountain. And when we got there a funk band was playing and we danced and drank as the place grew thick with bodies, the air dense with sweat and steam coming off coats and shirts and hats. That was the night Lindsey and Adrienne and I climbed up on the stage during a set break and started our own impromptu performance—I was on tambourine, Adrienne on maracas, Lindsey rapping, talking to the crowd.

Tom didn't drink much, because he had another plan. It was a secret he had told us, his sisters. At a little after eleven he slipped away and grabbed the backpack he had stashed under a table, changing out of his party clothes into his gear. Outside he had his skis and poles waiting, and then, in a headlamp and an avalanche beacon, with his pack strapped tight to his body, he began skinning up Mount Alyeska in the dark.

As midnight approached, snow began to fall, and I looked out the giant alpine windows up toward the dark shape of the mountain and saw it obliterated by flakes swooping down and catching the light and bursting against the glass. What strikes me now is that I was not afraid. None of us were afraid. While we danced and laughed and kissed, as the moment of the new year struck and rolled past, Tom was reaching the roundhouse at the top of the lifts. Then he turned and pointed his skis back toward us, onto the familiar runs, to become the first person to ski down Alyeska in the new millennium.

I'm trying to tell you that we all have the power to claim things. I'm trying to tell you that his record still stands. That it will stand for the next thousand years.

Acknowledgments

My first thanks go to the family members whose recollections provided this book's foundation and enriched it immeasurably. Thanks to my father, T.J., for supporting and assisting my efforts to tell this difficult story, and for his unwavering faith in me. Thanks to my sisters, Alicia and Adrienne, for helping me sort through my memories and feelings, for sharing their own, and for offering advice whenever asked. Many thanks to the aunts and uncles—Robert, Phelps, Barbara, Beverley, Sylvia, and Morgan (as well as Kit and Julie, both now deceased)—who answered my countless questions with honesty and generosity. And thanks to my mother, for her kindness and love.

This was a demanding book to write, about events that were themselves demanding, and it was clear to me early on that I could not manage it without consistent support. For that, I thank my husband, Will Palmer. It is not an exaggeration to say this book would not exist without him, for too many reasons to name, not least of which being that he acted as its proofreader. Thanks, too, to my stepchildren, Grace and Henry, for their cooperation in this effort and for all they are.

Numerous writers and scientists read part or all of this manuscript and offered their thoughts, insights, and criticisms. Thanks especially to Sarah Perry and Liz Blickle for their input, as well as many others in my Nonfiction MFA cohort at Columbia, who formed an enthusiastic audience for my earliest attempts to write about schizophrenia and whose feedback and friendship have been invaluable—Raina Lipsitz, Elizabeth Greenwood, Tara FitzGerald, Valerie Seiling Jacobs, Lindsay Wong, and more. Just as integral were the mentors who encouraged and guided those early efforts, particularly Patricia O'Toole, Cris Beam, and Lauren Sandler. Thanks also to the members of NeuWrite, and especially Carl Erik Fisher, for helping ensure that the scientific and medical information in these pages is accurate.

Thanks to the editors who first published versions of many of these chapters as essays in literary journals. Thanks also to copyeditor Susan Brown. Special thanks to this book's editor, Catherine Tung, for believing in what it could be and for helping it find its shape; and to my agent, Kristina Moore, for finding it a home. Their faith in my work has consistently exceeded my own.

I owe thanks, too, to the mental health activists who helped me explore my experiences among others who could relate, whose projects first provided me a platform, and whose conversations expanded and sharpened my thinking about mental illness: Rosemary Zibart, Maggie Jarry Atosona, and others at NAMI Santa Fe, Minds Interrupted, the Crooked House, and the Daughters and Sons Initiative. Thanks as well to Gary Travis for sharing his expertise on homelessness, to Annie Zak for helping me acquire my brother's court records, to Kass Atkinson and Katharine Dean for their excellent counsel, to Dianna Delling for the use of her condo, to Ben Anderson for his insights on architecture, and to the friends who allowed themselves to be named in these pages.

And most of all, to everyone who helped and cared for my brother during his years of homelessness, from the staff at Brother Francis Shelter, Bean's Cafe, Downtown Soup Kitchen, and Alaska Psychiatric Institute, to "Tom's cop," Wendi Shackelford, and the friends and neighbors who stepped in when they could, especially Sean, Kevin, and Zach: Thank you, thank you, thank you.

About the Author

Marin Sardy's essays and criticism have appeared in *Tin House, Guernica, The Rumpus, Fourth Genre, The Missouri Review, ARTnews,* and *Art Ltd.,* as well as in two award-winning photography books, *Landscape Dreams* and *Ghost Ranch and the Faraway Nearby.* She has also been the arts editor and editor in chief of Santa Fe's *Santa Fean* magazine. A Pushcart Prize nominee, she has twice had her work listed among the year's notable essays in *Best American Essays.* She lives in Tucson, Arizona.